keyhole

#11

Keyhole Press
www.keyholepress.com

Copyright © 2011 Keyhole Press. All content: rights retained by contributors. No part of this book may be used or reproduced in any form without written permission from the authors except in the case of brief quotations embodied in critical articles and reviews.

Editor	Gabe Durham
Associate Editor	Christy Chrutchfield
Associate Editor	Nick Kocz
Associate Editor	Brian Mihok

Cover photo by Jon Bergey, design by Peter Cole.

ISSN 1941-5362

TABLE OF CONTENTS

Kate Petersen / 4

Mathias Svalina / 13

Karen Pittelman / 20

Adam Cogbill / 24

Kate Wyer / 57

Fred Sasaki / 64

Sarah Malone / 89

Nate Liederbach / 105

Jonathan Callahan / 113

Contributor Bios / 148

THE CAVEATS
Kate Petersen

"I don't love you, but when I see your name I want to throw a refrigerator across the room," Melissa said.

"That's what he wrote? Show me."

"I left my phone at home."

"Okay, okay. My turn," Cail said. "I don't love you, but if you were a sports team I'd wear your jersey." Melissa unlocked the car and threw the movies in the passenger seat. It had been raining in earnest for the last two hours, hard, but they'd gone out anyway. "You will be the only one on the Ark who doesn't know who Myrna Loy is," Melissa had said. So they'd rented *The Thin Man* and *Petticoat Fever*.

"I don't love you, but how about beers?" Melissa said. The video store was down the street from a bar where Cail went to watch the basketball team she'd followed growing up. It was Saturday around two, and the day seemed long yet, unmarked.

"What about the meter?" Cail said. "I don't have any quarters." She was younger by eight years but had the more skeptical heart. Also, she had numerous parking violations in appeal with Somerville and felt she better understood the enemy.

"We'll build it into the price of the beers," Melissa said, and they ran across the street, holding paper grocery bags from the backseat over their heads.

The women shared an apartment, a teakettle and a pet turtle they'd found outside the Mexican place in Powderhouse Square. Moab, they called him, and when they couldn't find him they looked behind the dishwasher.

Besides Moab, it was just the two women, though men were always getting in their beds and first drafts then failing them. For Melissa, who had just turned 38, these failures were absolute.

"There's no time," she'd say. "The time I have is an imaginary number." Cail knew what she meant, but her dad worked as an engineer for NASA in the 70s and it secretly annoyed her when people used casual math like that, without understanding it, the way chain restaurants showed off their recycling efforts by listing how many cups went around the moon and back. The moon wasn't for stacking cups.

They sat at the front corner, near the window. The walls were hung with cityscapes made from backlit pushpins, and there was rock music on. They folded the wet paper bags and wedged them between the barstools.

"I don't love you, but my last three exes could be your sisters," Melissa said. She thought of Cail as she did her sisters, but it was a clearer affection, without the muddy obligation of family, the constant need to forgive or be forgiven. Sometimes it seemed it was Cail's age she loved, the great slack it gave her, to sit at bars alone watching a team no one in this town had heard of, or the way she laughed at too many things, like she would narrow it down later.

"I don't love you, but I am considering asking your sister out," Cail said.

"Don't say that," Melissa said. "Which one, Greta?"

"I'm joking."

"I know, but don't."

The apartment was in Melissa's name. It had belonged to her ex-husband, the divorce four years ago now, before she and Cail had met. Melissa had stories: Pills hidden in the drippings can in the freezer, and the second time he put his fist through the bathroom mirror Melissa left it like that, and only replaced it after he left. "It's like the Easter egg you find raking leaves," she'd said when Cail found a half-empty vodka bottle behind the winter coats. Cail admired the way Melissa moved about the things—not with any ownership or bitterness, but a sort of affection, as if she knew what they'd been through, left somewhere between dog-eared and worn.

"Brooklyns?" the bartender said.

"Two," Cail said.

There were two other men at the bar. One was grading papers and the other was watching the sports reel, shaking his head each time they showed the walk-off pitch from last night's game. A girl in a blue dress with an Asian collar was locking up her bike outside. She fiddled with a button at her stomach before coming inside. Melissa did that sometimes: it was a womb thing, and when Cail saw it she would go to the turntable and put on Otis Redding and they would dance, putting their shoulders in it.

"I don't love you but sometimes I pass off your theory of cooked raisins as my own," Cail said. Their beers came and they drank from them.

Cail didn't have any time either, though she tried not to think of it that way. It was not in her body yet, the wanting, but her parents were twenty years older than Melissa's—than everyone's—and Drew, the man she'd taken home to them had made good on his word of making a mess of things. There had been some mornings before that, though, an apartment with a big butcher block counter that Drew had built of scrap wood where they'd leaned before work, eating toast and listening to bicycles zip down their steep street the wrong way.

"I don't love you, but I'd declare you mine at customs," Melissa said. Lately, she'd begun to dream of friends' children: taking them to the post office and lifting them by the armpits so they could tape the letters closed, or walking along Crane beach and then going to the Clam Box after, wiping their fingers with wet-naps her dream-self kept in the car. She held her beer with her thumb and middle finger. This was what she might have to love in the end: the drama mask stickers on rented movie spines, a pale ale on an afternoon in fall. You had to start thinking what else would hold you.

"I don't love you, but it's one of my heart's FAQs," Cail said. Above their heads, the bottles were lined up. It went tequila-gin-vodka-rum-whisky-Scotch. Whisky bourbon, then Scotch.

"Damn," Melissa said. "I don't love you but good one."

"So did you write back to him?"

Melissa nodded. "I said save the fridge for New York next weekend."

Cail watched the man grade his papers. Melissa's refrigerator texter—Robb with two bs—was 30, and married. Cail did not approve, but you could only say so three times and then you were through. The second time she said it just like it was a fact, like the answer to a math problem you work back from: "He's married, Mel." They'd been talking on the porch where Melissa was painting an old tractor seat. "Jack says that's how they come now," Melissa said, straightening and pushing her hair out of her eyes. There was paint on her ear, but Cail didn't say so.

Now, Cail wished she'd gotten a bottle with a label to peel. The subject needed changing. "I don't love you, but when I saw you on my street, I thought you were pulling another white horse routine," she said.

"Really? Drew was on our street?" Melissa said. "When?"

"I was coming back from a run and it looked like him, locking up his bike, and he's done this before, at the old place, driven in from the blue, waited for me outside for who knows how long before work, just to walk me to the train." Cail held the beer in her mouth, let the hops spread their static over her gums. "Can I walk you to the train? he'd say. Like that.

"So I said hi and he said hi. And I think: Where would he walk me now? And no one moved—it was my turn, but I just stood there waiting for the arms or something."

"It's hard when you know exactly how much the arms weigh," Melissa said.

"But he just closed his bike lock, both hands, and said, I'm visiting a friend."

"On our street?" Melissa said. Cail nodded. "I don't love you," Melissa said, "but that's effing bullshit."

But it was Cail's fault for staying so close to the old apartment, where every street corner was taken.

"I don't love you, but what will I even do without you?" she said.

It was a real line, his. Their last morning, a summer ago, the one Drew had really come to walk her to the train. He'd been gone a year then, two hours west at school, and Cail had taken a new roommate when he left. She and Drew hadn't talked in months, couldn't seem to without tearing out the seams of the good years, but one morning when she came downstairs with her lunchbox he was waiting there on the sidewalk. His hands were in his pockets, and her bottom rib went funny when she saw him, the way it always had. He was in town for July, he explained, dog-sitting for his dad. They got as far as his father's street, halfway to the Harvard stop, then everything was the same: the fourth step that creaked, the shove of white light in the studio, the brushes drying in their peanut butter jar. Drew pulled the mattress he was sleeping on back from the easel. It was the slowest thing they'd ever done, and in the bright heavy after, he broke her heart finally. "What will I even do without you?" he said, tracing the question lines on her forehead. "Tell me what." Cail could hear the weak, improbable bells ringing in the Yard, and she didn't know, but she answered anyway. "A someday kid," she said. Touched the veins of silver in his beard. "Some lake towels and a paddleboat and you," a smile breaking in her voice, "will throw him off the dock," and her eyes washed up with the truth of it. The light came in whole through the window and made squares on them, bluing his freckles and eyelashes. The sheets had small interlocked squares too, and she was trying to remember it already: where her hands went on his back and his leg between hers and how he shook his head no in her neck, his hair getting in her mouth. "That was ours," he said. "I only promised to throw our kid off the dock, okay?" One of his tears fell on her face, and he wiped them away together, unfair as any last act is. "No putting words."

"Watch my wet paper bag," Melissa said, and left for the bathroom. A man and girl came in, shaking their umbrellas. She was wearing a shirt from the law school and he looked like he had driven in from somewhere, the top button of his shirt undone and sunglasses hooked where a tie might have been. He sat a seat away from Cail and she could smell the damp of his clothes, aftershave deepened by the rain. Cail set her glass down, keeping her hand flat against it as if protecting a flame. The man pulled some letters from his pocket and put them in front of the girl, who thumbed through them quickly without opening one. Permanent address. When Cail had called her parents to tell them Drew was moving out at the end of the lease, her mother had asked if she was sure. "He is such a gentle man, Cail," she said. "Onward and upward," her father said, his voice falling into one of the eight states between them. "Dad," she'd said. "So we'll see you at Christmas then," he said.

The girl ordered for them, pointing to something on the beer list. He asked her about class. She was probably close to Cail's age, except better posture, but he was young enough that Cail would have probably talked to him if it was just her and him and the game was on and it was a Thursday. She ordered another beer, picked at the layers of coaster bark. Her own father had lost most of his eyebrows in the last year, though his hair was still dark. She had noticed at the airport last time he picked her up; they looked like whiskers.

"I don't love you but when the upstairs neighbor comes home I call out, still thinking it's you," Melissa said as she pulled out the barstool again, shaking her head no when the bartender signaled for another.

"I don't love you, but it got close there," Cail said.

Melissa's mouth moved in big puppet-like increments, and now it bent into a frown.

"Greta's pregnant," she said. She lined up the base of her glass with words on the coaster, squinted if she were reading it through the refraction. "They weren't even trying." The rain was slant on the window.

Cail sipped from her beer and looked around for the girl in the blue dress. She counted the taps: they were all there. Greta was Melissa's sister, the one in Chicago, younger by five years. Greta had met her boyfriend six months ago. Cail could say something after three beers, but not one. Who knew what to say after one?

"I got this," she finally said. But Melissa shook her head wildly, finished her beer then tapped her wallet like it was a game show buzzer.

The bartender came.

"I don't love you, but I don't," Melissa said to him. He raised her empty glass at her before taking it away. "I don't love you either," he said.

"I don't love you," she said to no one, "but there are certain psalms."

The rain had become total. Melissa put dollars on the bar, and Cail put the ones she had down and put a glass over them. Taking their bags, they ran to the car and got in and drove into the thicket of rain, so much water that it seemed the sky was its own time, and day and night were lesser elements, so much that Cail told Melissa not to for the last time, knowing her warning would be lost in the great wash of sound: *He's married.* And Melissa went slowly around corners, Cail holding the movies in her lap, some radio song she half-knew nodding in and out under the din of rain like the promise your life makes without asking, and tells you so softly that by the time you finally hear it there is nothing to say but okay then. Yes, okay.

ICE
Mathias Svalina

"Joshua won't last two days," the cook said as he dug his fingers deep into the prone man's mouth. He grunted, then pulled out a jagged chunk of ice.

The cook handed the chunk of ice to Joshua's boyfriend. Joshua's boyfriend held the ice in his palm. He moved his hand in a small circle & the ice slid about on the layer of melted water. As it melted a red chunk embedded in the ice surfaced. After a while Joshua's boyfriend was only holding a small sliver of red flesh in his wet palm. It might have been a uvula.

That night Joshua's boyfriend fell asleep as he kept watch beside the bed. During the night Joshua's eyes froze over. By the time Joshua's boyfriend jolted awake the ice was so thick he had to crack it with a butter knife. He scraped the ice off of his slightly parted eyelids, doing his best to keep from ripping the skin up.

The next morning the ice had twisted Joshua's legs. His breath rose past blue lips in a weak mist that dissipated in the hot kitchen storeroom.

The cook found Joshua's boyfriend nodded out again on the stool & walked him to the break room, to the old couch. The couch smelled of fried things & dust. Despite the heat, Joshua felt cold. Without standing up he grabbed a handful of crisp, white aprons from the cabinet beside the couch & lay them over his body. He slept face down with his legs bent up under him & as the waiters & waitresses smoked their cigarettes they looked at him with pity. Yet they stayed on the opposite side of the room.

When Joshua's boyfriend woke his neck was stiff. It hurt to turn his head. He rubbed his left shoulder with the other hand & walked back to the storeroom.

Joshua was still on the wooden table, covered in blankets & coats from the lost & found. His lower legs, frozen solid, had both cracked off the body & one lay on the floor. They were beginning to thaw & a slow bubble of blood bloomed from each black tip.

After Joshua died Joshua's boyfriend walked out the restaurant doors into the coarse late morning sunlight. The sun rendered the empty strip-mall parking lot vast & violent. Accustomed to the dim kitchen, he could not open his eyes but the sun burned red through his eyelids. He raised his arms to the heat. He tried to absorb it all. When he opened his eyes he could see cold mist puff from his mouth as he exhaled.

He entered the first open bar he found, a narrow spot with a pressed tin ceiling. The old bartender stood at the far end with two old guys, all turned toward the color tv displaying a soccer game. Joshua's boyfriend sat halfway down the bar & hugged his arms into his chest. He looked toward the bartender but the bartender did not look back.

Joshua's boyfriend lifted the neck of his shirt over his lips & breathed into it to warm his chest. His spine shivered & his neck clenched. After a minute he slapped his hand on the bar. "Can I get a fucking drink over here," he said, his voice scissory.

The bartender & one of the other old men looked at him. The other man continued to face the tv, though it was only showing a commercial.

"A drink?" Joshua's boyfriend said. "That's your job, isn't it?"

The bartender wiped the bar with a white rag. "Tell me your wish, then," the bartender said. He had a Greek accent, maybe something more Baltic. "Let me hear it now."

"A whiskey. No, a double," Joshua's boyfriend said.

"The gift is only your beaten self," the bartender said, making no move toward the bottles of liquor behind him. "What grace have you brought to us?" he asked.

Joshua's boyfriend could not think of what to say. He widened his mouth & breathed slowly at the bartender, as if he was blowing a smoke ring. The cold mist emerged thick & white. He winked at the bartender.

"Your wish is burial." the bartender asked. "What of your life meanwhile? Have you forgotten that? Or do you care?"

The two old men were now standing behind Joshua's boyfriend. One had a baseball bat. The other had a crowbar. The bartender turned away from Joshua's boyfriend & walked through a red curtain into the back room.

Joshua's boyfriend put his head down on the bar. His face was cold against his crossed arms. He heard movement behind him. Something hit his left shoulder & his pain exploded. Something hit his head & he lost consciousness.

The shivering woke him. He could not make his teeth stop. The left arm would not move. Something crunched in his collar when he turned & pain electrified him, halting everything about him. He forced himself to breathe. The breath came in shudders from his lungs. The cold fog hung before his face.

He was in the weeds against a wooden fence in the alley behind the bar. His shoes were gone. He couldn't feel his feet, he realized, as he tried to stand up. His head rang with pain. He wedged his useless arm into the body of his shirt & began crawling with his one good hand. The cobblestones were slick with mud & grease & his hand grew black. He couldn't feel his fingertips.

He reached the sidewalk. His vision was blurry. The sun surged & the heat felt good. He lay down on a sun-baked spot of the street. The hot asphalt against his cheek felt like beach sand. Like when he used to swim in the cold water until his fingers turned blue & then lie in the hot sand & let the cold ease out of his body. The noises of other kids running & screaming around him. The ongoing mutter of the waves.

Joshua's boyfriend recognized the storeroom of the restaurant. All things were the cold now. The cook bent over him. He had a white rag tied over his mouth. Joshua's boyfriend could not move his body. Nothing but his eyes would respond.

"His eyes are open," the cook said. "And moving. Surprised they didn't freeze shut yet."

Joshua's boyfriend could feel the cook moving something around inside his nose. He could not feel it through the numbness, but whatever it was pushed his head this way & that. Finally the cook removed it, a thick pipe cleaner covered in red ice.

"I got as much of the ice out as I could," the cook said. "There'll be some bleeding, but that'll probably freeze up. Realistically, though, I don't seem him making it through the night."

"Oh, Joshua, you dumb little fuck," a voice said. A familiar voice, though tinny & off. "You can't die. Not now. Not when we're so close."

Whose voice is that? The speaker was outside his vision. Joshua's boyfriend tried to put a face to it, but he couldn't. Yet he knew it so well.

"They fucked him up real good," the cook said. Joshua's boyfriend could feel his body being moved, but he felt no pain as the cook touched his busted shoulder. "I'm going to turn him over," the cook said. "Get over here & help me out."

The mystery speaker walked over & Joshua's boyfriend could see that it was himself. He was wearing the same shirt he'd been wearing these past few days, ever since Joshua got sick. His eyes were red rimmed from tears & his face puffy.

The cook & the him turned Joshua's boyfriend over.

"Yep," the cook said. "I was afraid of that." The cook sniffled. Joshua's boyfriend rolled his eyes as far over as he could to try & look at them, but he could only see the shelves of canned goods.

"Once the ice forms on the skin like this, well, it's just a matter of time," the cook said.

There was a sound of crying, of sniffling, a whimpering. He recognized it, the rhythm of it, he could almost tell the next moment the him would sniffle again. He tried to sniffle, to see what it felt like, but his frozen nose would not respond.

KAREN PITTELMAN
Three Poems

I would be
deft cook
knuckles knived and burnt
making due with any
stalk or weed, all
versatile economy

But these
elemental salts
minerals that must be
mined—these the body
will not substitute.

So I sweep the backlots
weak-boned, bent
scouring the dirt, its
simple recipe:
two parts, bad wind
one part deplete.

Maybe our fathers were careless with the topsoil.

Maybe we have been forsaken
left to wander without even the comfort
of a golden calf.

Or maybe the forces of famine are just
indiscriminate, vast
rolling down the heat-shimmer plains,
a bitter sea.

Even now it brims, expectant
imagining itself some
bakery box trimmed
with red string I am
shepherding across
a crowded train

Ignorant as this moon
wrapped in pale, crepe sky
as if it were precious, as if we did not
turn our backs to it each dawn

So it seems that I mispriced
what is only
bulk, commodified
pork bellies or rice,
the heart no ineluctable organ
but something binned and
hauled by longshoremen
laboring in the dark—
a part among parts.

There is something ridiculous
about a chosen journey—
picnicked, portable
edged with the assumption
of home

Or am I only
envy, bent beneath
the weight of what I
could not keep, its slow drag
racketing behind me
like tin cans tacked by
heartless little boys.

I repeat the first rule of the refugee:
Do not catalog
Do not sit by the waters of Babylon
and weep

March forward.
And I do

I do, but still the
creeping
like some retinal disease,
mile upon mile
a small charred ache
scorched
all the way through.

EIGHTY-EIGHT BOOMERS
Adam Cogbill

Hello. My name is Vernon, and you are Boomer LXXX-VIII. I hope we can become good friends.

We have some things in common: we think swimming is great, but neither of us would enjoy the public pool. You're into circles, and I think that's nice. We can agree that circles are the Cadillacs of shapes. My sister, Penny, who is currently not speaking to me, can draw perfect circles without a compass. By this time you have no doubt observed the yellow and purple bruising covering the left side of my face, the stitches along my arm and above my eye, and you may even have noticed that, whenever I lean forward, I wince. This is because two of my ribs are cracked. Don't be concerned—the doctors have informed me that I will look like myself again in time. When I am uninjured, I am quite plain: I have short, thick limbs, and a face that is exceptional only in how unmarked it is by any significant flaw, coloration, or remarkable feature. Although it may appear that I am losing my hair, I must tell you that my hairline has been this way since I was fifteen. Fifteen was also the age I ceased to grow taller. Penny has said affectionately that I have the stage presence of a fire hydrant.

I have often wondered whether you or your predecessors understand me. The simple answer is, of course, absolutely not. Still, I must speak to you. I must tell you what has happened. You see, Boomer, I have spoken aloud to all of your predecessors. In doing so, I have discovered a calm unduplicated in any other area of my life. A more accurate answer then, is that you understand me perfectly. This is something I have come to understand about friendship: it has nothing to do with having palm lines that mirror another person's. You, after all, do not possess palms.

In a few moments, I must leave you, and I can't say when I will return. I know that goldfish have no use for explanations, but I offer one nonetheless.

Let me begin with the confession that there was a time when I believed myself incapable of causing anyone serious danger. When I say, "a time," I mean every day until yesterday. I was cleaning Boomer LXXXVII's bowl when it occurred to me that I have rarely failed another person, and that, rather than being an admirable trait, it is evidence that I have no one to fail, or that I never notice when I do. Consider how many Boomers I have lifted with the hand net and exposed to potentially deadly conditions. What kind of a person does not notice when he is risking a friend's life? And I cannot help but think that, had I failed my sister more often during the course of our lives, she would not have given up on me. I have spent my life avoiding anger and disappointment, Boomer, and I have gotten so good at it that now there is no one in my life I can disappoint.

You could say this began with Priscilla. In reality,

it began many years before. I have been falling in love steadily since I was nine years old. There was Nicole Swafford and Carlise Arnesse, Michelle Corelli, and Emma Bolton. When I turned thirteen, I surprised myself by falling in love with Mike Schmidt, and later, with Gabe Renshaw. It would be premature to say that I am bisexual. Think of me as enthusiastic.

I met Priscilla at an elegant Italian café that I went to because my coworkers, with whom I had declined to spend lunch breaks, discovered that I was instead eating at a foldout table in the janitor's closet, and began referring to me as "Stranger Danger." I knew her name was Priscilla because of her nametag. I noticed her before she came to the booth near the kitchen where I sat alone—where, for months after our initial meeting, I would sit alone—and I must confess, Boomer, that at first I did not think much of her. She was thick and shapeless, except for her head, which was long, and bore the faint and unfortunate resemblance to Burt's from Sesame Street. Her hair was the color of a rock's wet undersurface, and it remained in a motionless pile on her head and neck even when she moved quickly. Her nose was flat, and when she focused on you, her eyes took on a noticeable squint, as if your appearance was, to her, unfathomable.

But then, Boomer, I saw her carrying a cup of espresso. How incredibly she moved! When I hold out my open hand, my fingers quake and shudder, but Priscilla's hand was as steady as the stroke of a swan's wing. The surface of the espresso was unbroken by her steps, the cup completely still in its place at the center of the saucer. She did this effortlessly, with no need to pay attention to her hand or arm. And I felt, as I had so many times before, desire begin to set in. I have come to recognize it as one recognizes by the sky's appearance an impending rainstorm . When I feel this way, I speak, if at all, on autopilot, and I am aware of my own body's movements only after they have happened.

When she arrived at my table, she stood with her hands behind her back and looked at me pleasantly. "Something to drink?"

Her voice was rich. I was certain her laugh rivaled theatre sound systems.

"I said do you want something to drink?"

I hated espresso—much too bitter—but what else could I have said, Boomer? To see her emerge from the kitchen with that miniature cup and saucer embraced in her fingers...I nearly ordered two.

It is good that I did not, as I was unable to finish the one she brought me. I was forced to empty the cup in one of the restaurant's large potted palms when no one was watching. When she returned to find my cup empty, I was rewarded with a long look at her hand as she replaced the cup and tiny spoon on the saucer before lifting it to her tray, which she balanced on the fingertips of her other hand.

"Can I bring you anything else?" she asked.

I wanted badly to say, "Yes." Instead, I said, "I am okay."

I returned to the café on a near-daily basis, either on my lunch break or post work, and after several weeks I had learned her schedule and the tables to which she was nearly always assigned by the manager, who, I noticed, had a habit of holding his hand against her waist or arm while speaking to her. For a time, she greeted me by saying, "How have you been?" to which I was only able to respond, "Fine," and stare at her until she realized I was not also going to ask how she had been. After a while she stopped asking and, upon approaching me, said only, "Espresso today?" The only change in our routine over those months was that I learned to stop scrunching my face in revulsion when I drank espresso. This felt to me like overcoming a great obstacle, and I enthusiastically related my triumph to Penny. We had maintained regularly scheduled telephone calls since she moved several time zones away with Charlie—a large, friendly man unaware of the force of his own backslaps. They married last year, but I was unable to attend the ceremony because I would have had to travel by plane.

Penny responded blandly, "Just think, Verno. If only you'd put that much effort into liking Priscilla, you could be telling her how you overcame your fear of espresso."

"I am working on it," I said.

"You could be on an actual date. At this very moment. You could be—what time is it there? Eight? You could be walking out of a restaurant together right now. You could be panicking about whether you should take her hand. Wouldn't you rather panic about holding hands?"

"She has lovely hands."

"I know it's a novel idea for you, Verno, but just try and find a way to tell her you like her."

I had considered this. By, had considered this, I mean, had considered this to the point of hyperventilation, which I concealed, when at the café, with frequent trips to the bathroom, which I covered by telling Priscilla—though she never asked—"Coffee is a diuretic." We rarely spoke other than to address the business most pertinent to my being seated in her section. Mostly, I sat and watched her take orders, enter and leave the kitchen, or converse with the manager. You might wonder, Boomer, if I was really happy in this limbo. I am unsure. I can only say that had it not been for the actions of the manager on an otherwise unremarkable Wednesday afternoon, I would probably still be visiting Priscilla.

When I think or hear or say the word "manager," I will forever be reminded of this manager. He was an aggressively tanned man with a severe comb-over and a stomach that extended so far from his body that it appeared to be a separate entity; when he spoke, it waggled not with his voice but in response to it, as if it were at all times agreeing with him. His posture was so stiff that, when he was standing still, he leaned backward. He compensated for this when addressing customers by bending forward at the waist so that his rear jutted out behind him like a turtle extending its head from its shell. He was long-limbed, a trait I now associate with people who are constantly correcting those around them. He chastised his staff openly, in full view of the dining room, and he often offered advice to customers, suggesting that they might like something other than what they ordered. And the touching! To him, there must have been no distinction between people and merchandise in a department store. He had no qualms about laying his hands on his customers' shoulders or on their backs, grasping his by their chins and hands. His hands seemed always to be reaching in particular for Priscilla, resting on her shoulders and wrists, dancing near her face. I developed toward him a seething, adamant jealousy.

I had gone after work that day, as I knew by then that Priscilla's Wednesday shift was always in the evening. Except for an elderly couple whose clothes matched—khaki pants and mustard colored sweaters—and two men in suits with glasses of wine in front of them, the place was empty. I sat in my usual booth near the kitchen doors. The café was lit by small oil candles set on each table and by three large chandeliers on what must have been the dimmer's lowest possible setting. While I waited for Priscilla, I counted the burned-out bulbs on each chandelier. The manager, his face as blank as a paper lunch bag, thumped across the floor toward me, and for a moment I feared he might intend to burden me with some suggestion. But he continued past as though my table were empty. He positioned himself at the elbows of the men in suits and began an unprompted exposition on the wine list.

Priscilla emerged from the kitchen, carrying above her left shoulder a tray with two plates of something red and steaming. In addition to her normal blue and black uniform, she wore a thin, bright yellow headband. She smiled at me—she had grown accustomed to seeing me—before heading, with her tray, toward the elderly couple at the back of the café.

As she was passing, the manager performed his rear-extending stoop maneuver, and Priscilla received the impact squarely in the hip. She was flung sideways, the tray tipped from her fingers, and the plates were slung directly at the floor, their contents remaining remarkably still until the moment of impact, when they shattered. Bolognese splashed everywhere. Pieces of porcelain skittered along the tile past my table.

There was, for a moment, the kind of silence that results after a tragedy during which everyone silently estimates how much damage has been inflicted. The primary casualties were Priscilla's uniform, the manager's trousers, and various nearby tablecloths. Priscilla had taken the worst of it; Bolognese clung in chunks to her apron and fell like drool down her shoulder and leg. pattern on her ankle resembled a bell. Her yellow headband was unmarked. For a moment, I thought to stand and offer my napkin, to wipe the gunk from her neck, to dab at her hands.

The manager turned to Priscilla and opened his mouth. His top lip quivered as though trying to detach itself from his face. He thrust a finger toward her and shouted, "You stupid"—here the quivering temporarily ceased, and he looked momentarily confused before rediscovering his voice—"clumsy, fat fool! Look what you've done!"

He berated her for being careless, called her incompetent and awkward. I sat up straight in my seat. To say that Priscilla was clumsy, awkward! To suggest that what had happened had been in any way her fault! I found myself clenching the tablecloth in both fists. The manager thrust his hands in the air as though throwing open a pair of drapes. It was then, Boomer, that I made up my mind to come to her defense. I would cause him serious danger. I stood up, removed my wallet from my pocket, placed five dollars on the table for the espresso I would've ordered and the tip I would've left, and made for the door.

I went immediately to the post office where the only pay phone remaining in my town is located. I inserted two quarters and dialed the café's number, which I'd long before committed to memory. After a moment, the hostess answered.

"Good evening," I said, doing my best to make my voice into a deep rumble. "May I speak with the manager?"

She said that she would get him and asked for my name.

"Tell him that it is an old friend."

After a moment, there was a rustling on the line, and then I heard the manager's voice, still tinged with irritation. "Can I help you?"

"Actually," I said, "I'm calling to help you."

"Excuse me?"

"When you speak, you sound much less impressive than you believe."

"Henry? Is that you, Henry?"

"You are the sort who constantly re-shapes his beliefs to match his desires, and therefore your beliefs mean nothing."

"Who is this?"

It was too late to stop, Boomer. I said, "Given the choice between you and a jar full of dog flatulence, I would take the jar." I hung up before he could say anything else. I was not an experienced anonymous caller, but I was fairly certain that successful anonymous calls end with the anonymous party hanging up first.

You may imagine Boomer, that as a child, I was a lonely outcast. I wish I could surprise you and say that this was never true; that some other, tragic set of circumstances caused me to become who I am, but I cannot remember a time when I was situated in or near the social center of any group of people. As a child, I played almost exclusively a game that I referred to as "Fugitive," in which I imagined that I was being pursued by an organized, terrifying, and violent agency of unknown allegiance. I imagined this agency to be multinational and possessing the most advanced tracking and surveillance technologies. I imagined all pedestrians were agents, passing cars were driven by agency operatives, and birds and cats were highly advanced reconnaissance drones equipped with cameras shaped like eyeballs. I had no particular conception of why I was being pursued, nor did I know exactly what would happen if I were caught, but I could not imagine a more terrible fate. I hid in hedges, crawled under fences, avoided sidewalks and roads. Always on the lookout for secret hiding places, I was delighted by trap doors and crawl spaces. I loved tree houses, and I knew the locations of half a dozen within a several-mile radius of my childhood home.

At school, "Fugitive" became a much less imaginary experience. I was the target of bullies and teachers who believed shy children should be forced from their shells. I preferred math tests to group projects. I feared lunch and the moments immediately following the last bell, when children were left in a mostly ungoverned mass, and when certain children were prodded with protractors, bombarded with pencil shavings, kicked in the rear, had their backpack ripped from their back and emptied in the middle of the hall, and were hip-checked into lockers and girls they were in love with. Penny was my lone ally. She accepted this role without complaint, and performed it unwaveringly. When we were in our early twenties, our parents were killed in a gas explosion, and except for Penny, my communication with other people was limited to returning clerks' greetings at the grocery store, or thanking the librarian for processing a book.

I returned home an hour before Penny was expecting my call, but I did not wait; I wanted badly to share with her what I'd done. While the phone rang, I did laps around my kitchen, running my free hand along the counter. I looked at the clock. It was nearly nine where Penny lived. She would be ensconced on the sofa, legs stretched at angles that would cause the average human being immense pain, a novel open across her thighs. She would look irritably at the phone—perhaps she would yell for Charlie to answer—and then, after three rings, she would resentfully toss off the blanket or sweater she'd covered herself with, stalk across the room, and—

"What is it?" Penny answered.

"Blake One!" I cried.

Penny and I share the middle name Blake, and in playful moods, refer to each other as Blake One and Two respectively.

"Vernon?"

"Affirmative, Blake One."

"This is a nice surprise. You never call early."

"Something has happened," I said. I nearly told her right then, but then I remembered that when we speak to those we love, we must follow certain protocols. So I asked, "How is Charlie?"

"What? He's fine. What happened?"

"And Sparticus? Has he eaten anymore of your books?"

"I moved them all to higher shelves. Vernon, tell me what happened!"

"And what about your—"

"Vernon!"

I told her. I began with the yellow headband and did not stop until I got to dialing Penny's number an hour earlier than scheduled. She was quiet for the entirety of the story, and remained that way after I finished. I counted twelve-elephant, and then I said, "Penny?"

"I'm sorry," she said, although she did not sound sorry. "Can you tell me one more time what the point of your prank call was?"

"It was for Priscilla?" I had not intended for my response to sound like a question.

"I don't see how this helps Priscilla."

"Oh. That is because that is not all there is to my plan." I waited until it became clear that Penny was not going to ask me to explain myself, and then I explained myself. "I am going to call again tomorrow. And the next day. And the next. And—"

"This doesn't make any sense." There was something bitter in Penny's voice, something I couldn't recall hearing before. "Vernon, just tell her you like her. Isn't that what you're really trying to do?"

I could not answer because I had inserted the collar of my shirt into my mouth and was solemnly chewing it.

"God. How long have we been having this conversation?"

This was a question I could answer. "I have been visiting Priscilla for three months, two weeks, and a spare Wednesday."

"No, I mean—or yes, you have, but we've been having this conversation longer than that."

"I apologize for not understanding."

"Do you remember Nicole Swafford? Back when we were in high school?" Penny asked.

She already knew I remembered Nicole Swafford. What she really meant was, I have something to tell you something that you should've known since Nicole Swafford. Boomer, why does so much of what we say mean something we are not saying?

"Do you ever wish," she went on, "that you'd told her how you felt about her?"

Penny has a constellation of moles on her right shoulder that she claims would resemble me if I were obese.

"I have never wished that."

"Oh come on, Vernon. Don't you wish you'd tried, at least?"

"I thought you would be proud of me."

"Proud? That instead of functioning like an adult, you're making prank calls?"

"It was not a prank," I said. "It was a very serious anonymous call."

"You know what the legal term for 'serious anonymous call' is? Harassment. You're harassing him. I think you could be charged with a felony."

Sometimes, Boomer, sometimes when I consider what I've been taught about family—which is that while they may cause a person's blood pressure to fluctuate wildly, a person's care for them should be as steady as the EKG of a coma patient—I wonder if the lesson's purpose is to teach love or to keep us safe.

"Promise me you won't do it again," Penny said.

Boomer, I refuse to say that I do not know why I lied. When we say we don't know why we did something, what we really mean is, what I did now appears to have been the wrong thing to do. So: I lied because, although I did not intend to stop making anonymous phone calls, discussing the situation with Penny made me feel like I was trying to do somersaults across the surface of a pool.

"I promise," I said.

"You are without a doubt my favorite brother, Blake Two."

"I am your only brother."

"Still. When am I going to see you next?"

"You are always welcome. I will put clean sheets on the foldout bed."

"The foldout has a bar running down the center exactly where a normal person would put her spine."

"Then I will take the foldout and put clean sheets on the bed."

"My point is, you could come here. You could take a train, you know. You don't have to fly."

I was unable to respond.

"Never mind. That's not such a good idea either. I'm sorry Vernon. I'll try and take some time off next month."

"I'm sorry that you always have to be the one to travel, Blake One."

"The things we do for love, right?"

For her tenth, eleventh, and twelfth birthdays, I gave Penny jars of pennies I'd saved during the previous year. I did this because beginning on her ninth birthday, Penny said she would no longer answer to Geraldine, which was her given name, and that she preferred to be called "Penny."

I am, in some respects, one of the most fortunate people I know. I have never in my life been without someone to speak to; Penny had always been there when I needed her. But after we hung up, I felt alone. Before I lied, I had imagined us as two equal halves of a circle. After I lied, I thought of us as a half circle and a half rectangle jammed together. Then I began to think of other lies that existed between us. After she joined the high school softball team, I told Penny that I had a developed a moderately severe allergy to leather so that she would stop asking me to play catcher while she practiced her fastball. I do not think she found out that this was a lie. Do lies accumulate, Boomer? Are we always becoming slightly more misshapen?

After I'd hung up, I wandered the house. I rearranged cupboards that were not in need of organization; I scrubbed surfaces that were already clean. I was reshelving my books alphabetically by title when I was visited by a notion—one that became increasingly entrenched the longer I considered it—that some of my books preferred not to be positioned next to each other. No matter how diplomatically I spoke to them, they seemed to be inconsolable. I was compelled to promise one that I'd find it a more agreeable spot, and soon I was surrounded by small stacks of books for which I could not find acceptable places. I began to sweat; I plugged my ears. After a while, I determined that remaining alone in my house would be impossible.

I do not attend church services, but I do enjoy fundraisers: bake sales, canned food drives, cakewalks. Etcetera. These events are usually full of people who are friendly and at ease. That night, the church down the street was holding a carnival to raise money for new hymnals. I successfully popped a balloon with the third of three darts at a distance of fifteen feet, and in return I was awarded a goldfish in a water-filled plastic bag bound with a rubber band. I christened the goldfish Boomer.

Boomer—known to me now as Boomer I—was killed when, as I was walking home from the church carnival, I set his bag down to tie my shoe, and an apparently unchaperoned child with a running start chipped him into the street, where he was squashed by a passing pickup truck. I could not think of anything to do but go directly to The Pet Place, a pet store near my home, the following morning, and purchase a new goldfish, who I named Boomer II.

Boomer II died due to a lack of proper goldfish care knowledge on my part. I assumed: fish, bowl, water, food. I assumed: deposit a handful of food in the bowl and gauge an appropriate amount for future meals based on one night's consumption. Later, when I found her belly up, I realized my mistake: I had no way to measure how much she'd eaten. You should know that I am rarely this careless, and I always learn from my mistakes. Eighty-six Boomers later, I am an experienced and skillful feeder.

Boomer's IV and V died because, I discovered, even trace amounts of dishwashing liquid can be fatal to fish if not entirely wiped from the bowl. I made anonymous phone calls to the manager each day for several weeks. I disguised myself as a representative for a food distributor, or as a customer who wanted to complain about the previous night's meal, or as someone in search of a job. I began to practice false voices at work, in the shower, in front of whichever Boomer. Sometimes the manager answered the phone himself, in which case I told him simply that it was "a friend of a friend." I could usually get in a single sentence—I would tell him, "You are in no way worthy of managing other people," or, "Your world has the depth of a child's wading pool," or, "Your presence taints the atmosphere of your establishment with inhospitality"—before he hung up. Occasionally he demanded to know who I was, or threatened that when he found out, he would commit horrible acts of violence to one or more of my various body parts.

I continued going to the café in person—it might've seemed suspicious to disappear just as the anonymous phone calls began—and though I often wanted to tell Priscilla what I was doing, I was no more able to do so than to ask to see her outside of the café. When Penny asked about Priscilla, I changed the subject. Penny had a habit of knowing when I am not telling the entire truth, and I was certain if we spoke for very long she would've discovered what I was doing. My relationships with both Penny and Priscilla contained some amount of deception. I believed I was keeping all of us from serious danger.

I was halfway through a sandwich and an espresso. The weather had turned cold, but the café was tenaciously heated. Even with my jacket off, I could feel perspiration accumulating along my hairline and beneath my arms. One of the servers had dragged a chair over to the door and was standing on it to wipe a high window with a cloth. I could see Priscilla cleaning the soft drink machine in the server's stand. A radio played loudly in the café's kitchen, and the manager had just stalked past me for the second time to tell the kitchen staff to turn it down.

As he came strutting back, his stomach preceding him like a truck leading a float in a parade, he let his eyes fall to the half-eaten sandwich on my plate and he stopped abruptly. He ran one hand gently over his comb-over, as if testing for static, and peered down at me. For a moment, Boomer, I feared that he might vomit. Then, clasping his hands behind his back, he asked, "Is something wrong with your sandwich?"

"No," I said. "It's correct."

"What?"

"I mean, it is fine." I was unable to look at him. He began a half-speed version of his rear-extending stoop, and I wanted desperately to check to see if he was inspecting my sandwich or me.

"It's just that you don't seem to have finished much of it," he said. His voice was a hiss.

"I am taking my time."

He recoiled a few inches, and I was suddenly sure that he knew who I was. In a panic, I spoke again, this time injecting as much rasp into my voice as I could. "Everything is okay here," I said, and then, because he did not alleviate the silence with a response, "I am enjoying my meal."

The manager's eyes went wide, and he leveled a two-finger point at the center of my forehead. "It's you," he said. He lifted his head as though looking for reinforcements and proclaimed, "It's him!"

The hostess and several of the servers had stopped what they were doing and peered in our direction. The manager performed a small leap. "You're the crank caller!"

I pulled my wallet from my pocket, emptied the cash on the table, and dodged around the manager, who lunged at my neck and missed. I made my way through the tables toward the door. I heard the manager come crashing after me, kicking over chairs I'd sidestepped, knocking silverware to the floor.

As I passed the soda machine, I chanced a look at Priscilla. I wish, Boomer, that I had not. She is fixed in my mind that way: pressed against the soda machine, the lemon lime lever, depressed, soda was pouring out, her long fingers splayed over her mouth, and her lump of hair jammed between her skull and the machine's logo. I had the impression that her knees buckled slightly, so that she looked on the verge of sliding onto the floor, but I also remember that the look on her face was more outraged than afraid, and what I thought of as buckling could have been her preparing to spring at me should she receive the opportunity. Her face covered almost completely the cursive letter "o" in the well-known soft drink company's logo.

The manager may have stopped chasing me to at the threshold of the café. I didn't look back to find out. I never saw Priscilla again.

At home, my heart beating the rhythm of spooked and stampeding cattle, I dialed Penny's number. She answered on what I knew was the last ring before her answering machine picked up.

"Something has happened," I said. "Something bad."

I heard her rearrange the phone against her ear. "Tell me about it," she said.

I told her how I'd continued to make prank calls, about the manager recognizing my voice and chasing me from the café. When I was finished, I was gripping the phone with both hands and my eyes were jammed shut.

"Vernon," Penny said.

I waited. I expected her to yell at me, Boomer. Penny is quick to raise her voice. It is one way I know that she has been thinking about what I've told her.

"Vernon," she said again.

"I am listening," I said.

I could hear her breathing, which was slow and controlled. I began to count elephants, but stopped when I went past twenty-five.

"Blake One?"

"Things can't go on this way, Vernon."

"What cannot go on which way?"

Boomer XX died of broken bowl due to alarm clock-induced morning slapping. Bowl moved to bathroom.

"You. What you do. How you are."

"Do you think if I saw her on the street, she would greet me?"

"I want you to listen to me carefully."

"Maybe it was not that she was afraid of me. Maybe the uproar of the chase frightened her."

Boomer XXVI died of what I can only imagine was goldfish cardiac arrest. I found her belly up after a night in which the apartment complex at the end of the street caught fire and a large part of the night was sirens and screaming.

"I am going to hang up the phone," Penny said.

"Do you think once she has had some time to think about it, she will arrive at the conclusion that I have done something admirable?"

"I won't answer if you call me back. I won't return your calls."

I was twisting back and forth the knob that controlled the gas to the stove's front left burner. "Maybe she has already thought about it."

"We will not speak until you have a meaningful interaction with another person. Make—"

"What if she is looking out the window right now, waiting for my return?"

"Make a friend. Go on a date. Volunteer to read to children. Anything."

"Penny," I said. "Do you remember when you gave Chuck Stanley a black eye? For throwing each of my shoes into the top branches of a different tree? And how after, when I tried to thank you, you punched me in the stomach?"—I am sure, Boomer, that by the time I'd said this much, Penny had already hung up—"This is something I often think about. I believe now that you were trying to help me, somehow. I frustrated you. And though we have always said that we could tell each other anything, the truth is that we only say what we are not afraid to say. So you hit me—"

I was interrupted by the busy signal. I stood with the phone pressed against my ear and listened to it blare.

I was envious. How effortlessly a busy signal communicates with anyone who can hear it.

"Because," I continued, "of what you could not say to me."

I read that goldfish adapt to the size of the environment in which they live, and the fact that I kept Boomers XL through XLIV in a small outdoor water-filled pit may have contributed to their enormity. I eventually became weary of the required upkeep, and all subsequent Boomers lived in fishbowls like this one. Plus, I caught Eisenhower, the neighbors' cat, making off with Boomer XLIV dangling from his mouth. This possibly explains the disappearances of Boomers XL-XLIV.

I did call Penny back later that night. She did not answer. I tried again the next morning, still without success. Penny has always kept her word, and I knew before each attempt that there was little chance she would reconsider.

Over the following weeks, I fell in love in semiautomatic bursts. A woman whose hair was an electrified, frizzy sculpture jogged by my window, causing me uncontrollable joy for brief seconds before she turned a corner and broke my heart. A dog-walking gentleman in his late fifties handled his Newfoundland courageously, but could not manage a smile for me. In the grocery store, a flock of college girls in bright pink shorts made my chest feet tight and fluttery until their laugh were too many aisles away to hear. I felt cast aside when the clerk at the corner gas station only handed me change and looked to the next customer. A woman with a warrior's stride flung open the doors to the local bank branch, but was followed by a boyfriend. Librarians killed me—those dimples! those hands! Fellow bus passengers made me sweat.

Boomer, if I were asked by anyone but you why I began making friendships, I would have said that it was to satisfy my sister's demands. But in truth, I began making friendships because I could not take falling in love with so many people.

Let me disclaim that these friendships would not have satisfied my sister's definition of "friend." "Friendship" here refers to any exchange or a series of exchanges with another human being. All unaccompanied persons in public locations were targets for the making of a possible friendship. I liked to imagine that whatever chemicals are generated by the making of a friendship leave residue in the location where the friendship was made, and, if one had the capability, one could recognize the chemical signatures of friendships I created all over my town.

I said to a man while we waited for the bus, "Do you think you'll need that umbrella today?"

He said, "I certainly hope not."

The previous is an example of a single-exchange friendship.

I said to a woman in line at a department store, "That's quite a lot of pairs of socks you have there."

She was searching through her purse and did not look up. "My kids go through them like you wouldn't believe," she said.

"I would believe."

"It's like they ingest them. I have no idea where they go."

At this point, she picked up one bag of ankle-high athletic socks from her cart and held it toward me. Boomer LIX experienced what I sometimes believe to be the most tragic death of all the Boomers: having had too much with a new friend, whose name I never learned, at a local bar, I knocked his bowl out an open window. I have never entirely forgiven myself for such grossly inappropriate behavior. Please know that although you currently inhabit the 7th fish bowl I've owned, this one has lasted longest. And I have mastered the art of placing fishbowls in locations of least potential harm. I thought the woman might've wanted me to take the package of athletic socks from her and examine it more closely, so I reached for it, but she dropped it back into her cart.

"How much do you think these things cost to make?" she asked.

"I don't know."

"Well I don't either, but I know how much they cost to buy." She made an expression that I am sure was meant to suggest that the price of socks was excessive, but which actually looked as though she were struggling to defecate.

The cashier cleared her throat and said, "Did you have trouble finding anything today?"

I said, "I did."

The cashier looked at me. "Are you two together?"

"No," I said. "But I momentarily had trouble finding the light bulbs." I waved my package of light bulbs at her to show that despite my difficulty, I had eventually tracked them down.

I considered both of the people involved in the previous exchange to be friends.

I took Boomer LXXV on a picnic and fell asleep. I was awoken by an unleashed dog with its snout in Boomer's fishbowl. Boomer LXXV was gone. The dog's owner was nowhere in sight.

I fed Boomer LXXXIV from a canister of fish food that was recalled two weeks after her death and a week before the death of Boomer LXXXV.

I arrived at The Pet Place to purchase the goldfish I would eventually name Boomer LXXXV on the morning of the season's first snow fall. It'd been several months since I'd heard from Penny—by far the longest we'd gone without speaking to each other. The Pet Place was staffed, that morning, exclusively by Ray, whose name I knew exclusively because of his nametag, and who you, Boomer, may remember as the heavyset individual with skin as pale as an albino's, so thin that his vascular system was visible. There was often an open, half-eaten bag of sour cream and onion potato chips near him. I had never attempted to make Ray even a single-exchange friend. Normally, he was equally content to ignore me as well. He was always reading while he worked, and when he scanned my purchase, he looked up from his magazine or book only as much as was required to operate the cash register.

As often as I had been there, I did not find The Pet Place an agreeable place. It was full of adjustable metal shelving stained by a mysterious brown substance. It smelled overwhelmingly of wood chips and feces. The tile floors were a shade of yellow that looked grimy even after a recent mopping. The only window—a large one at the front of the store—was obscured by a mural of various types of puppies interacting with a huge red ball, so that the light that made it through window was blended into a dark, demonic red. When I considered the hamsters and rats, the birds looking out from between the bars of their cages, and the puppies and kittens in their enclosures, I was disconcerted by the thought of what would happen to these animals if they were not purchased.

Because Ray was the only staff member working, I was forced to request that he retrieve the goldfish I selected. Wordlessly, he scooped it from the tank, placed it in a plastic bag, and bound the bag with a rubber band. I left several feet between us as I followed him to the cash register. I had the idea that if I got too close to him, some integral part of me could suddenly change into something unrecognizable.

We completed the business at the checkout counter in silence. I kept my eyes on the box of specialty dog treats shaped like gingerbread men until I heard him mumble, "So, what happens to these goldfish, anyway?"

I veered back toward the dog treats. "What do you mean, 'happens'?"

"Special treats for your cat? Drop them down garbage disposals? Whack 'em with golf clubs?"

I felt the way Wile E. Coyote must when he looks down and realizes there is nothing below him. "They are my companions," I managed.

"Okay," he said. He tapped the fingers of his right hand in rapid succession on the countertop. "Except that a well-cared for goldfish can live ten years. You're in here every couple of weeks."

"I am doing my best."

"I'm sure that's comforting to your fish."

The bag dangled heavily against my leg. "I admit," I said, " that I sometimes fail my friends."

Ray curled his fingers into a fist, which he brought down like a gavel on the counter. "I guess I know what you mean about that."

I had the suspicion, Boomer, that whatever he thought I meant was not what I meant, but I responded with what I hoped was an encouraging nod.

"Look," Ray said. "What's your name?"

"Vernon."

"Ray," Ray said, tapping his name tag once. Then he extended his hand. His skin had the consistency of wax paper. I took it with my own mostly because I was unsure what else to do.

"One time I knocked a guy out of a moving pickup with a hiking boot," Ray said.

"Pardon?"

"I know. I had gone camping with some friends. We were taking the back roads home, and a few of us were riding in the pickup bed, finishing up the last of the bottle we'd brought. Had our shoes off. Just relaxing. And this guy, Beaver we called him, he tells me that a few months ago, he and this girl I was seeing at the time had had a little too much fun one night. So I picked up my boot and threw it at him. Hit him between the eyes, and he went over the side of the truck."

"Quite unfortunate," I said.

"He's okay now. Mostly. Married, has a kid. Sometimes he says things out loud that he meant to just think. Pisses off his wife."

"Friendship is a dangerous thing," I said.

Ray lifted a trash can from somewhere beneath the checkout counter and spat into it. "You be good to that goldfish, Vernon."

I assured him I would. It did not occur to me until I left the store that I had no idea how many exchanges we'd shared.

When I returned several weeks later and reported that Boomer LXXXVI had suffered a fatal confrontation with a raccoon, Ray rolled his eyes and accompanied me to the goldfish tanks.

"Let me ask you something," he said as I leaned in close to the tank to inspect its inhabitants. "If, every day, at an unspecified time, somebody showed up wherever it is that you were and gave you a harsh kick in the junk, would you rather that somebody be someone you knew or a stranger?"

I straightened too quickly and bumped my head against the glass of the fish tank. Ray appeared to be serious. "Would it be the same stranger?" I asked.

"No. You'd never see the person coming. And you can't ever dodge the kick."

"What if I became proficient in martial arts and—"

"No!" Ray said, chopping at the air with his hands. "You must get kicked in the junk, you never see it coming, and there's no way to soften the blow. Come on, Vernon. Someone you know or a stranger?"

"I suppose I would prefer a stranger. I would not like to expect my friends to hurt me."

Ray crossed his arms and nodded. His eyelashes were so light they were nearly white. "See," he said, "I'd want it to be someone I know. In fact, I'd want it to be a friend. Or even a family member."

I was unable to respond.

"The way I see it, if space command has to take daily direct hits, I want it to come from someone who understands what I'm going through."

"Space command?"

Ray poked me in the chest. "Yeah, Vernon, space command. The Red October. The goods. Keep up. Anyway, what I'm saying is, if it's a good friend, you can probably get over him kicking you in the balls. Because he's probably kicked you in the balls a few times already, and you have some practice getting over getting kicked in the balls. Right?"

"I don't know. I don't have many friends," I said.

Ray considered this. Then he said, "Well, Vernon, I'll be your friend."

"I would like that very much," I said. Then, because there seemed to be nothing else to say about the matter,

I pointed at a goldfish with white, feathery fins and said, "What do you think of this fish?"

Ray squinted. "You got a name for her?"

"Boomer. Boomer the eighty-seventh."

"Hey," Ray said. "Sure. I guess that makes as much sense as anything else. Tell you what. Promise me you'll take care of this one, and she's on me."

"I am not sure that is a promise I can keep, considering my history with goldfish."

Ray shook his head. "I'm not asking you give her a good, long life. That's not something you can promise. I just want you to intend to give her a good long life."

I nodded once. "I will try."

So, Boomer, I left The Pet Place cradling your predecessor, Boomer LXXXVII, to my stomach, and with the knowledge that I had possibly made a friend. You may imagine—and correctly—that as I stepped off the curb, I was, for the first time in months, remarkably content and unaware of the tribulation that the world often visits upon us. I have no memory of being struck by the bus. I am told I was thrown twenty feet before landing on my side and rolling onto my face near the curb. In my most optimistic moments, I imagine the fate of Boomer LXXXVII to have been resolved quickly.

My stay in the hospital was uneventful. I was mostly immobilized, and I spent a great deal of time on perception-altering substances. I thought a great deal of Penny, who I did not call; she wouldn't have answered the phone, and I did not want to tell her machine what had happened. More importantly, I was worried she would immediately buy a plane ticket, and I did not want her to see me in such a condition. She would've blamed herself, Boomer. I also thought of Ray, to whom I had made a promise to keep your predecessor safe, and who I had miserably failed. I believed this was the reason he did not visit me in the hospital. If it is possible for a friendship to be measured by the pain one feels after failing a friend, then, despite our brief acquaintance, Ray had a significant impact on me. I believe, Boomer, that love is a way of distinguishing those who we are most willing to put in serious danger. I wonder, then, if it is not better to be alone.

This morning, I returned to The Pet Place to apologize to Ray. He wasn't there, and I approached the store manager—a short, sweaty woman who repeatedly dragged her forearm across her forehead as we spoke—when he would be working next.

"Ray doesn't work here anymore," she said.

"I see," I said. "Do you have a way I could contact him?"

She was struggling not to stare at the bruised portion of my face, which had taken on the color of molding peach.

"Ray passed away," she said

"Passed away?"

"Heart attack. His third."

I stared at her. Her khaki shirt had two breast pockets, and after a while, she became fascinated with the button on the left one. Then I said, "I'm sorry."

She shrugged. "Too many potato chips, I guess."

I was unable to respond, Boomer. I left her and went over to the fish tank, where I met you.

Even small toothpick crosses take up a lot of space if there are enough of them. In fact, if you ever visit my backyard you'll notice that nearly half the space, including the area by the fence where I used to plant tomatoes, are resting places for Boomers.

I've done some research: they will not allow me to take a goldfish on an airplane. Not under conditions conducive to goldfish survival.

I know that you cannot understand this. But I must try to explain it anyway. Boomer, you are my friend and I must put you in serious danger. I am going to visit Penny, and I cannot bring you with me. I will buy my ticket this afternoon. I have never been on a plane and do not know what it will be like. I am scared, Boomer.

I asked my neighbor, Mrs. Bennington, who I met for the first time yesterday, if she could feed you. She seems quite nice; she said she would be happy to. When I return, I will discuss the details of my trip, including the quality of airplane food and the furniture my sister has but cannot afford. I will think of you while I travel.

Good-bye, Boomer! I am going out into the world despite the kind of place I know it can be. I will leave the radio on.

KATE WYER
Stand Up, Step Apart
A Run
Voice, Lost

STAND UP, STEP APART

"Come here by the water," she says. He listens. He crouches next to her and waits. She places her left hand on his knee and dips her right hand into the brackish water. She brings her fingers to his forehead and makes a downward movement, then brings them back up, retracing the wet path before adding a horizontal line.

They stand up, step apart. He wipes his forehead with his sleeve.

"I undid your baptism," she says.

"That's bullshit," he says, wipes his forehead again, still feeling a slight damp there. He touches the place with his pointer finger, rubs it.

"You can't undo it like that. You gotta do this," he grabs her wrists and pulls her into the cold water, drags her in up to her waist.

She is laughing and shivering. She pinches her nose shut and he takes this as his signal to push her head under the water. He holds it there for a moment, feeling the roundness of her skull in his palm, before releasing. She surfaces, dark hair over her eyes in thick clumps, like eels. She pushes it out of the way and slaps the surface of the water.

"A common heathen!" she proclaims. She moves towards him, ready to reciprocate the ceremony.

"No," he says. "No," his head a dim unholy nothing.

A RUN

He says, "You're not good at this."

She thinks he means driving, so she straightens her posture, checks her mirrors and her speed.

He sees that she doesn't understand. "No, sitting with people. You're too nervous."

Of course she is—pulling her ponytail tight to her scalp, tying knots into the frayed bits of her cut-offs, wiping the oil off of her nose with her sleeve. It's just a comment, she thinks, not a judgment. He looks at her like it is a judgment, though, like he expects her to talk as part of his fare.

It's not exactly polite to ask who her passengers are going to visit at the maximum security prison. Or how long their person will be there. Or, of course, why their person is in jail in the first place. People will sometimes volunteer the who and how long but almost never the why. Sometimes, though, the family member believes their person is innocent. Then she learns too much.— winds up shaking her head in frustration as they tell their story.

Since he is asking her to talk, it's the only thing she can think to ask. "Who are you going to visit?" The most harmless part of the triad.

He shifts in his seat a little. A truck with a horse trailer pulls up next to them and then away. He watches a proud chestnut rump shiver a fly. The black and white pony next to the thoroughbred pulls up and down on his bit.

"My son's friend," he answers. He runs a ringed hand over his shaved head, rubbing the crown a few times. She has inferred tattoos onto his covered arms. The dress shirt he wears seems too large, it swells with air from the open window.

"This is your business, right? I mean, you started this," he gestures to the interior of the car and then vaguely towards the door, where on the outside panel is her removable decal.

"I own my own daycare," he continues, "it's lot of work to only make 20K a year."

"I can't imagine," she says, and she really can't, but tries to, and sees herself in the center of a room with a rainbow on a wall, a jumping and smiling frog and some clouds. She is alone in the room, though, no kids.

"Why?

"Why do I run a daycare?" he answers. "Lots of reasons, I like kids."

It was funny to her, the way people either liked kids or really didn't like them. The ones that didn't like them said they hated them even. She did not belong to either population. She opened her driver's side window and put her forearm on the sill. The sun was weak.

"How old are your kids? Like, yours, not the daycare ones," she asks.

"Twenty, eighteen and twenty-five." She wonders why he didn't list them in chronological order.

"It's the twenty year old whose friend I'm going to see."

She nods.

"William," he says.

"That's your son?"

"Yes."

The cab feels bigger now. She notices her breathing has relaxed and allows her shoulders to settle back onto the seat. It's also her favorite stretch of road on the trip. The road opens up and slopes down through corn and soy fields. They both let the wind blow in the cab, feeling like they had done something good, made some kind of human headway. The horse trailer was a few paces ahead of them and made for entertainment, even if the horses weren't doing anything. As the road curved, the horses' tails swayed a little to the side. A box truck pulled up next to the trailer, pacing it.

Now they watched the two vehicles—the box truck cutting into the lane of the trailer on a bend around a hill. The box truck hitting the side of the horse trailer and sending it over.

She stops, puts the car in park on the Interstate. He is already out, at the back gate of the trailer. He pushes the latch in and down and the door swings with gravity towards the road. The horses are wild, their bits knotted to the front of the cage. He presses in beside the pony, presses past angry, frightened kicks. He loosens their bits and they back out, tossing their heads. The horses are running the road, leaving the road, they are breathing foam. She stands in the road, waiting.

VOICE, LOST

Samantha often swore to God.

Until New Year's, that is, when she lost her voice due to a bad head cold. No more strained stories of lost cell phones that had text messages from Dr. House (I swear to God) or neighbors climbing naked up fire escapes (Seriously, I swear to God).

Everyone suddenly liked her. The silent Samantha at her desk, silent Samantha in the ladies room reapplying lip balm, silent Samantha leaving to smoke without anyone noticing.

The week progressed like this until the shock of her voicelessness wore off. It was as if the foul-mouthed Samantha had never existed; everyone forgot to wait for the voice to come back. Samantha had obviously recovered, no more tissues or red, peeling nostrils.

Yet no voice.

The voice was quite happy. It was hanging out with all the other lost voices in the bar for lost voices. The voices marveled at her ability to swear, especially to God. Voices are very superstitious. If a voice hiccups, everyone in the vicinity shouts, "God bless you!," so the voice's heart won't stop. The others liked her quite a bit and described to her what they thought her body would look like; especially the mouth that the voice came out of. "I'm not from New York. I'm from Connecticut. But, yeah, I went to public school. No, I don't wear lipstick, I swear to God—no! I don't scream when I..." She was the center of attention.

Samantha went to several doctors. They couldn't explain the loss and wrote more prescriptions for cough syrup with codeine. She texted obsessively. But texts are easy to ignore and the friends who had hung around waiting for the time to ditch her, ditched her.

Meanwhile, the voice was getting on every one's nerves. She really was too much and they were tired of being shocked. The old barmaid had connections to a voice that knew people. Money changed hands and it was arranged that the first available person would get Samantha's voice. The bar folk followed Mucinex purchases on their BlackBerries and made bets. They hoped for either a man or a nun.

The voice started to clear her throat. "Hum, HUH!" And again. They giggled in anticipation and drank up. She cleared her throat once more and was gone.

Samantha got a promotion at work. She finished everything too quickly and had loads of time left over, so she created a foundation where celebrities spoke about her rare condition. In six months she was able to quit work and go on a book tour.

The voice passed into a thirteen-year-old Haitian boy living in Washington D.C. He was considered clairvoyant and all the neighborhood kids came to ask him about their love lives. He was more than happy to dish.

FRED SASAKI
Intuitive Reading
Schaumburg Flyers

INTUITIVE READING

PART 1

From: Fred Sasaki
To: Penny Slusher
Date: Sun, Jan 23, 2011 at 2:56 PM
Subject: Intuitive Reading

Hi

***

From: Fred Sasaki
To: Penny Slusher
Date: Mon, Jan 24, 2011 at 8:43 PM
Subject: Intuitive Reading

Hello?! I'd like to schedule an intuitive reading please.

Thank you,

Fred Sasaki

***

From: Penny Slusher
To: Fred Sasaki
Date: Mon, Jan 24, 2011 at 9:55 PM
Subject: Intuitive Reading

Hi Fred

Thanks for contacting me. I'd be happy to set up an appointment with you. May I ask how you heard about me?

I'm in Chicago - but also do some Saturdays at Buzz Cafe in Oak Park - I will be there this Saturday the 29th from 6:30 to 9ish.

If you're in Chicago or are open to coming to the city, I have some time open next week. Let me know what works for you and we can take it from there.

Penny

***

Fred Sasaki
To: Penny Slusher
Date: Mon, Jan 24, 2011 at 11:48 PM
Subject: Intuitive Reading

Hi Penny,

You're welcome! Thank you.

I'm wondering why you didn't know how I heard about you, but it also sounds like you intuited that I got your card at Buzz Cafe. That's pretty good! I also looked up Intuitive Reading on your website and was confused at first but now I think I get it. It is all about intuiting! LOL!

How do we get started? Do I say what I want intuited, or do you tell me?

Fred

***

From: Penny Slusher
To: Fred Sasaki
Date: Tue, Jan 25, 2011 at 6:45 PM
Subject: Intuitive Reading

Hello Fred,

Let me explain a little about my readings so that you understand how I approach them.

I'm not all-knowing or all-seeing. If I were, I would play the lottery and I'd be rich and would know everything that's going to happen.

It doesn't work that way. Here's what I CAN do. I can sit down with a person and tell them what I feel is near them or coming to them (as far as events, people, or most importantly - life issues or blocks that may be keeping them from moving forward). The life issues are what I put most of the emphasis on and they are much of the focus of the reading. I often have a sense of what the person I'm reading might be feeling - that's why I call my readings "intuitive".

On occassion, I may talk about things that would be considered prognostications. It is really a matter of what I pick up on in any given reading. I compare it to turning a dial on a radio....whatever comes through, comes through. I don't have much control over the content.

I may touch on the one burning question or problem you are wondering about in your life - and I may not. Again, it depends on what "comes through". If I don't pick up on something in your life that you want to know about, you can ask me about it - but it is nearly impossible to give a definitive yes or no answer. I can give you my first "gut reaction" in regard to the question.

What's important to me, is that each person I read gets something from it that they can use in their lives. I can tell you this, that, and the other in a reading but the person is really in control of their own lives - nothing I tell them is set in stone. The reason for that is because each of us has free will.

So if you are interested in a reading, we can make an appointment and if you want to ask me to focus on one issue or area of your life, I can try to do that. OR, you can simply show up at the time of the appointment and I will tell you what I "see" for you. It's really your decision.

I hope that helps.

Regards

Penny

***

From: Fred Sasaki
To: Penny Slusher

Date: Wed, Jan 26, 2011 at 5:18 PM
Subject: Intuitive Reading
Hi Penny,

I am not interested in getting rich quick if that's what you mean. That's for hooks and fienders. Though maybe you don't win the lottery because you also know how your closest friends and relations would turn on you like butcher vultures. Or maybe the drinking and drugs and other loose ways would cost so much more than a fortune. My mother always said that about the lottery and about feeling bad for people who win it and their tragedies. She also said to never wonder what drugs feel like which I hadn't thought about till she mentioned it. Also about the hooks and fienders.

I am at a real place of decision. What I do next could mean something, or go this way or that way or the other way. But I do not know except that it will probably be something. I have a lot of life issues for you. I would also like to know more about free will. That seems very important in everything I am writing.

One thing before anything else is a story about intuition that I would like you to read and see as a sort of fecundation. When I was 15 years old I rode my bicycle by the lake. I was overweight and lonely with no friends except Paul McCartney LOL! I would ride my bicycle and think about getting thinner so people would like me and I wouldn't be embarrassed about wearing T-shirts or not wearing T-shirts or about jumping around or being touched. I had a really nice bicycle. I won't even tell you how nice. My father spoiled me and bought me the best bicycle I could ever have, which was actually a really bad bicycle for me to have. My mother would scream Why are those people looking at your bicycle like that!? People judged my father and me for having such a nice bicycle.

Anyways I loved riding that bicycle and taking care of my bike. I had a little tool kit and everything. One day I was riding and I remember I was wearing my Paul McCartney concert T-shirt and I rode by Fullerton Ave and the lake. Right at the scary part someone at the water fountain yelled to me for help. I stopped because I thought I was helpful, and that I should show the world and the man who needed help that I am not racist against black people. I asked what was wrong thinking I can fix it, but he kept coming closer and insisting that I get off my bicycle and sit on his bicycle so I can see what is the problem. I started to inch away because I intuited something wrong but he grabbed my bicycle and said Get off I have a gun in my pocket. I jumped off and he rode away. As he rode away I yelled after him, Please sir! Someone who saw the whole thing came back and asked me Did that guy just rob you? I said Yes and the guy said I thought so. He was not helpful at all. Then I went to the police with the thief's bicycle to make the report. The policman was black, too. He said, Was the guy black? I said Yes even though I didn't want to bring it up. He asked How tall was he and How much did he weigh. I had no idea. Basically someone taller and thinner than me. I figured he was as tall as my father, so I said 5'8". I figured he must weigh a little less than me, so I said 180 lbs. The policeman said, So he was a short fat guy? That really sucked and then the policeman took the bicycle the thief left, as evidence. I walked home.

When I got home I had to buzz in but my mother was in the bathtub. I buzzed and buzzed and she let me in. She said she could tell something was wrong by the way I buzzed. I told her what happened and she hugged me and I cried and she blamed my father for the bike being too nice and then said that the man was a nigger and that was just what he was a nigger. That made me feel really bad because then I was guilty twice. Later the kids made a lot of fun of me for believing anything at all.

That's a long story but it's really a short story if you think about it. There is a lot of intuition in it and a lot of not listening to intuition. Things can be so different. Is that what you mean? By the way, this is not what I want you to read about me in real life.

Fred

***

From: Penny Slusher
To: Fred Sasaki
Date: Wed, Jan 26, 2011 at 11:27 PM
Subject: Intuitive Reading

Fred,

Thank you for sharing. Would you like an appointment? My fee is $20 for 20 minutes.

Penny

***

From: Fred Sasaki
To: Penny Slusher
Date: Wed, Jan 26, 2011 at 11:49 PM
Subject: Intuitive Reading

Hi Penny,

You're welcome. I'm glad you loved the story. It's all true. I would like an appointment but I think we will need at least two hours to start. For such a long time we will also need to eat food and drink coffee or wine. If we drink wine we will need even more time because I get really excited and talk a lot about a lot of different things when I drink wine and one other thing. Do we take time outs for going to the bathroom and eating? Because if we meet for 2, 3, or 5 hours I will spend at least twenty minutes total in the bathroom if not more, especially if we eat a meal with dessert not to mention coffee. Then there is all the chewing which takes up time too.

Let me know how you handle the rates and I'll block out time on my Google calendar.

Thanks,

Fred

***

From: Penny Slusher
To: Fred Sasaki
Date: Thu, Jan 27, 2011 at 12:37 AM
Subject: Intuitive Reading

Fred

I think you misunderstand the nature of my readings. I do not go beyond 30 minutes with readings. If it's conversation you need, you will have to meet with a friend or family member. I don't spend more than 30 minutes with any client. I don't socialize with clients. Thank you for understanding.

***

From: Fred Sasaki
To: Penny Slusher
Date: Thu, Jan 27, 2011 at 10:36 AM
Subject: Intuitive Reading

Hi Penny,

I understand. There is no need to thank me. But I do not misunderstand. I simply didn't know about your half-hour time limit. Do you prorate the ten additional minutes, making it $30 per half hour? This may be a silly question, but given that we're on the subject, do you take off time for bathroom breaks? Also, do you book back-to-back appointments?

And while I appreciate your offer for conversation, that is not what I'm looking for. I have many friends and some family to talk with about things. My social calendar is full already and I can't afford to add to it. I'm not looking for a social partner, no offense. But if you like I can provide feedback, or what I like to call instant analysis, on our session. We can call this service Instant Karma. I can give you insight to what you're doing, how you're doing, and make recommendations for the future. My fee is small as I feel one incurs bad Karma for charging too much for Instant Karma. $15 per half hour is my fee, but I work on a sliding scale. That's only fifty cents per minute! But we can sort that out after our session. Please note that I also offer complementary trail Instant Karma sessions where the client owes Karmically, and not necessarily to me but the universe.

Let's not get too far off subject, though. What days of the week are best?

Thanks for understanding,

Fred

***

From: Penny Slusher
To: Fred Sasaki
Date: Thu, Jan 27, 2011 at 6:45 PM
Subject: Intuitive Reading

Fred

At this point, I feel as though I'm not a suitable person to do a reading for you. I recommend you try to find someone other than myself. I won't be able to tell you anything useful. I can tell I'm not going to be successful in giving you a good reading. Sometimes that happens. I wish you luck in all you do.

Best regards

***

From: Fred Sasaki
To: Penny Slusher
Date: Fri, Jan 28, 2011 at 11:35 AM
Subject: Intuitive Reading

Hi Penny,

Well, it's starting to sound like this isn't going to work out. Maybe with some practice you will be able to be able to give more readings. Would you like me to send your free trial Instant Karma report? That might be very helpful. Let me know.

Fred

PART 2

Evite Invitation:

You're invited to
Penny Slusher 50th Surprise Party & Flash Mob!

Hosted by David Kropp

A Flash Mob?

Hey, we've got the skills, we've got the guts ... why not? Instead of the usual, tired chorus of "Surprise!", when Penny heads home we'll pose as theatre or restaurant patrons, then reveal ourselves in song. The music and movement will be simple and fun ... but something cool that Penny will always remember. Details to follow.

P.P.S. Friends with musical and choreography talent to stage our Flash Mob, please contact me.

***

From: Fred Sasaki
To: David Kropp
Date: Tue, Mar 29, 2011 at 8:40 AM
Subject: Penny Slusher 50th Surprise Party & Flash Mob!

YES!

Hi David,

I am really excited! And I'm nice to meet you. Hopefully we won't be too much competition for each other, former partner! LOL!

So I have a lot of ideas for the party. Also I have a lot of stories for you and Penny and the guests. What fun!

First off, I LOVE your P.P.S.

First things first. Did you say FLASH MOB?! LOL! That is my specialty. As a former theater person myself, I know how to raise eyebrows and heartbeats and expectations and the sexy level of any situation. Let's get up and at them! My first thought is something Chippendales. I can do a little dance or dance routine. Maybe I can do "I'm Too Sexy" for Penny like in the old days. Right Said Fred! I can strip off a little bit, get the people hot and bothered, and whip it around like a towel. I can do the helicopter twirl spin which is kind of my speciality. Or just a hula hoop.

OR...

I can do my cocktail waiter striptease routine. I think you know what I mean :) This won't interfere with your cocktail waitress unless you want me to. That is extra spicy. OK! Let me know how you want to plan this out. Here's "MY SONG"!

Right Said,

Fred

http://www.youtube.com/watch?v=39YUXIKrOFk

***

From: Fred Sasaki
To: David Kropp
Date: Fri, Apr 1, 2011 at 11:36 AM
Subject: Penny Slusher 50th Surprise Party & Flash Mob!

Hey David,

What's going on? I'd like to get planning things.

Thanks,

Fred

***

From: David Kropp
To: Fred Sasaki
Date: Fri, Apr 1, 2011 at 11:41 AM
Subject: Penny Slusher 50th Surprise Party & Flash Mob!

Couldn't get the facilities for April 9th.

Party to be moved to a different location on a different date. At least 1 week later than planned.

Will keep you posted.
D.

***

From: Fred Sasaki
To: David Kropp
Date: Fri, Apr 1, 2011 at 12:40 PM
Subject: Penny Slusher 50th Surprise Party & Flash Mob!

Wow ok. My lips are sealed. I'll still show up at the said date just in case there is lots of confusion. Sounds good?

***

From: David Kropp
To: Fred Sasaki
Date: Fri, Apr 1, 2011 at 1:31 PM
Subject: Penny Slusher 50th Surprise Party & Flash Mob!

Actually there is something you can do to help. We need people with cars to transport those without wheels.

Please give me your address. I will plot you on Google maps and pair you with the closest people.

D.

Sent from my BlackBerry

***

From: Fred Sasaki
To: David Kropp
Date: Mon, Apr 4, 2011 at 1:59 AM
Subject: Penny Slusher 50th Surprise Party & Flash Mob!

O my. Seeing this is a drinking dancing party I am not driving anywhere! Where will the party be? Perhaps this is a case for a limousine? I took one recently to Great America and had a great time. My friend's girlfriend threw up in the car but it was OK. The driver was really nice about it.

What do you think?

Fred

***

From: Fred Sasaki
To: David Kropp
Date: Mon, Apr 4, 2011 at 12:29 PM

Subject: Penny Slusher 50th Surprise Party & Flash Mob!

Hey David,

I just checked in to the Evite and there is no new information or anything. I am starting to think you do not like my ideas. That is fine, even though my feelings are hurt. If you don't like me or like the great plans I have for dancing, I don't have to do them. That is no water off my head.

Let me know about the limo or not. Either way I think I am too sad now to have fun at Penny's party. I won't tell her anything of course, but when you see her tell her I did my best. O well. But if you change your mind and still need someone with choreography talent (me), let me know and I'll bust the moves.

Thanks I guess,

Fred

***

From: Fred Sasaki
To: David Kropp
Date: Fri, Apr 8, 2011 at 11:56 AM
Subject: Penny Slusher 50th Surprise Party & Flash Mob!

Hey David,

Just checking in to see if you've changed your mind about tomorrow night about the dancing. And do you still need rides? I'm rethinking driving since I'm not going to be going all out with my I'm Too Sexy routine. Unless you want me to. Either way, like they say. AC/DC! LOL!

Fred

SCHAUMBURG FLYERS

From: Fred Sasaki
To: info@flyersbaseball.com
Date: Sunday, Oct 17, 2010 at 11:27 PM
Subject: Schaumburg Flyers

Dear Schaumburg Flyers,

I would like to come in to try out for the Schaumburg Flyers baseball team and fulfill a lifelong dream of playing on the field. I should say in advance that I am not a very good fielder, but I have a great hitting pose. In high school I played every position. In the outfield I had trouble catching fly balls. In the infield the grounders kept hitting me in the shins. First base was no good because I am really afraid of the ball and pitching was just dangerous. So I mostly played catcher but that didn't go so well because I couldn't throw all the way to second base and I'd miss catching a lot of pitches. People stole home on me all the time, which frustrated everyone especially the pitcher. I am a good hitter when I actually hit the ball, but I'm still afraid whenever the pitcher throws it, which makes it a little nervous. But I definitely look good in a baseball uniform. That and I'm a lot of fun in the dugout. I'm also 34.

Do you need to know how fast I run or how much weight I can lift because I can figure that out.

Thanks,
Fred Sasaki

***

From: Scott Boor
To: Fred Sasaki
Date: Monday, Oct 18, 2010 at 8:50 AM
Subject: Schaumburg Flyers

Fred

Our open tryout will be in May check back with our website after the new year for more information.

***

From: Fred Sasaki
To: Scott Boor
Date: Friday, Oct 22, 2010 at 9:50 AM
Subject: Schaumburg Flyers

Hi Scott,

Excellent. So you think I've got a great chance at this? I do too. I've been thinking for a long time now to find a new career and this just might be the thing. Put me in touch with the coach so we can have brunch or even just breakfast. I'm a healthy eater.

By the way, is uniform number 3 available? I'd like to be no. 3 since it rhymes with Sasaki. The people will find it easy to remember this way. I'll be totally popular like those other Japanese players.

Wow. This feels good.

Thanks,

Fred

***

From: Fred Sasaki
To: Scott Boor
Date: Friday, Oct 22, 2010 at 9:52 AM
Subject: Schaumburg Flyers

PS. I'd also like to do commercials.

***

From: Fred Sasaki
To: Scott Boor
Date: Monday, Oct 25, 2010 at 3:05 PM
Subject: Schaumburg Flyers

Hi Scott,

    I thought a lot about baseball over the weekend and talked to my parents about my new career a little bit over lunch and then dinner. My father always thought I could be a professional baseball player! My mother is of course upset and depressed about it but she is always depressed and upset about a lot of things. You should have heard her when I said I wanted to be a carpenter! Or an actor! Or luxury hotelier! Or a writer! Or go into advertising! Or film making! Or teaching! Or anything, really, now that I think about it. I think she wanted me to be an engineer. But she always wanted me to be something I am not. Like she is really upset that I don't think I am white. She thinks I can SAY I am white if I FEEL like I'm white. Of course I FEEL like I'm white but I do not LOOK white. Of course I look whiter than say, Barak Obama, but my mother says Barak Obama isn't even black. She says that he is NOT the first black president. Isn't that funny? She also says Tiger Woods isn't black and that it is really terrible that everyone should try to MAKE him be black. I sort of look like Tiger Wood, if you know what I mean.

So let me know what's up. Shoot me the coach's phone number, preferably cell.

Thanks!

Fred

***

From: Fred Sasaki
To: Scott Boor
Date: Tuesday, Oct 26, 2010 at 3:41 PM
Subject: Schaumburg Flyers

Are you guys getting my messages? Scott?

***

From: Scott Boor
To: Fred Sasaki
Date: Tuesday, Oct 26, 2010 at 4:20 PM
Subject: Schaumburg Flyers

Fred

I am getting your messages. As I mentioned our tryouts are next May. Please look for the tryout application on our website in 2011

Thanks

***

From: Fred Sasaki
To: Scott Boor
Date: Saturday, Oct 30, 2010 at 1:01 AM
Subject: Schaumburg Flyers

So Scott,

What I want from management is a little encouragement.

My father has always been very encouraging to me even though it's more a sort of delusion. He wanted me to be an archaeologist. In kindergarten I stood up in front of the class and said I wanted to be an archaeologist and everyone was impressed. We loved Indiana Jones. Later my father said I would be a great businessman. One time he told a customer at his store that I was in business school at Northwestern. I don't know why.

I had to say, "No, that's not true. I don't know why he said that." When I won $40 at a casino he said I could be a professional gambler. When I wanted to do magic he let me burn things and put a table cloth on a table and put glasses and plates on top and practice yanking the cloth out like magic. I didn't break anything. Now he says I will be a famous writer and I should have my own column where I say things. I guess what I'm getting at is that he always let me have magic.

Now I'm bringing that to you. I'll see you in May.

Fred

SOCIAL UTILITY
Sarah Malone

Gerrit was fortunate in his desk. From it he could see the ocean-going ships enter and exit Rotterdam harbor, seeming about to ram the Erasmus Bridge until it lifted and they slid through. Often, eating lunch, he watched the next hour's weather slant in from the North Sea and the tall cloud shadows cross the red and orange freight containers while his floor-to-ceiling windows shook.

Meike, his girlfriend, would call or text by one. She was an advertising account executive a few kilometers away in a district of converted warehouses. During the workday, a few minutes were all she could spare, and her voice skidded to a stop.

"Guess what I'm doing."

"Giving the prime minister a massage."

"Funny Gerrit. I'm thinking of you. Will you be in all day?"

Of course he would be. He returned to his computer smiling, fingers blurring across his keyboard. He managed investments for a government pension fund—like the engineers of coastal flood barriers, making the country safe to ignore him.

Meike emailed a few minutes later. Hug was underlined. Click. A page opened on his screen: Welcome! Your friends are just a keystroke away. This again.

Meike's favorite "social utility," as she called it. For months, she'd been telling him to join. Everyone in her office had joined. Everyone who joined got his or her own page and could read the pages of any friends who had also joined.

"So it's everyone I already know," Gerrit had said.

"But what are they doing this instant?"

She'd showed him her page. Meike is tired of fish, it said at the top.

"We don't have to eat fish," Gerrit said.

"I only wrote that to make people smile." She'd mussed his hair.

The page her email opened was clean: a logo, a few buttons and lines of text—no legal backtracking, no question where to begin, its authors clearly thinking of people who lacked Gerrit's knowledge, his skill. But it was free to join. And he still had a half hour of lunch. He typed his email address in the box labeled 'email' and entered his first name as a nickname. A nickname was required. Yes, Gerrit did want to search his emails for friends who were already members. Thirty! Odd that no one had mentioned it. But Meike knew every trend early, as she knew which movie stars were sleeping with one another, and the latest slip-ups of politicians. "Part of my stupid job," she said.

Would Gerrit like to find anyone for whom he did not have contact information?

Katarina. His mouth still had the name ready. Ridiculous. He could never have said he really knew her. Her sister, Anneke, had been in his year in school, short and shortsighted, with dark curls and hands like rolls of dough on a baking sheet, the kind of girl you could poke trusting her not to read more into it. Katarina was the year ahead, slim, just tall enough not to scare off ordinary boys; round-faced, with a baby nose and bounces of golden hair, and a way of giggling that made people think they were witty. And riding boots every day. "Like a good melon," Maarten Oosthuizen had said. "Half the fun is getting past the rind." Gerrit didn't know about that. Katarina must have married years ago. She would never have had trouble finding a man, or a woman. Gerrit had mainly seen her at school musicals and choir recitals. She was second soprano and always got minor parts. He'd joined stage crew just to speak to her.

"Good luck," he remembered saying, before the curtain rose on the first act of the fall play. He was in tenth grade. They were standing in the wings, stage left, close enough to whisper.

"Thank you," she'd whispered.

The social utility brought up four entries for her name, one in the Netherlands, two in Germany, one unspecified. The Dutch woman wasn't Gerrit's Katarina—too angular, though pretty, in a thin way. The first German woman was too dark-skinned, the second one too old. The fourth woman had no picture.

Meike called as promised, as soon as she'd finished with her client, and by six-thirty her and Gerrit's bicycles were locked outside the apartment block she'd chosen the summer before, a tidy brick building in a new district along a canal now used only by kayakers on weekends. Beyond the canal, a motorway ran behind a low sound barrier. Gerrit would have preferred a modernist building in the heart of the city, but they had to choose from what was affordable and available. He'd felt blissfully magnanimous, yielding. They were going to live together! And she was paying two-thirds of their rent.

In their cheerful kitchen—blonde cupboards, yellow walls, and, in the window alcove, a tall narrow table with a green tile top, all Meike's choices—she was opening white steaming cartons of take-away Chinese. She had on deep purple lipstick. When she tilted her head her straight, black-dyed hair, cut just above the chin, fell free on one side.

"It's fun, right?" she said. "Finding people?"

"I may try to find some people from school," he said.

"I want to see all your old flames."

Of course she was teasing. But she had shown Gerrit her school pictures, and he'd met the blade-sharp men from her office, toned and slim, with house-shares on the Costa del Sol and ski chalets in Gstaad and film-shoots in Chile and Baja that were a chore even to mention. Film-shoots were chores, Meike said. She never wanted to do another. Waiting nine hours for five minutes of shooting, after flying six thousand kilometers—no thank you!

Gerrit could picture the conversation if Meike saw Katarina's picture. She'd want to know who the pretty one was, and he'd have to say Katarina's name as if it were like any other. But if he showed nothing, Meike would be free to imagine, and what if she imagined he'd had no friends at all?

After dinner, she paged through a loud celebrity magazine and he brought his laptop from the bedroom. It was pleasant, facing across the kitchen table. Usually she was in the living room emailing or texting co-workers while he washed the dishes.

"Have you noticed how all the famous people are friends?" she said.

"Who else can they be friends with?" Gerrit said.

"But they're all famous for different things! How do they meet?"

"How does anyone?"

Gerrit typed the password to the government pension database.

"It just seems lonely." Meike put down her magazine. "Imagine we were friends."

"Friends?"

The database returned nothing for Katarina's last name—surprising since every citizen had an account, and the database checked married and maiden names.

"From school," Meike said. "If I became famous, how would you feel?"

"What do you mean, how would I feel?" Gerrit felt he was being tested on something she wasn't asking.

"If people are close, shouldn't what's between them be the only thing that matters?"

"What if you move apart," Gerrit said, "and enough time passes that if you meet, neither of you are who the other one remembers? What if you have nothing left to say?

"People always have things to say," Meike said. "It doesn't matter if you're close."

She stood up.

"Do you ever want to lose people instead of find them?" Gerrit said. He felt her chin on the top of his head.

"I can't believe you're the one who brought work home," she said.

"It's nothing," Gerrit said. "Five minutes."

He heard her open their bedroom door. He typed, first name only. Katarina. The database returned too many names to sort. As it should be. Katarina would live her life. She would give or take orders in an office, have children, worry about their falls and feign amazement at schoolyard sagas until a new face eroded from the round cheek Gerrit had seen from the wings as he mouthed her lines.

Other classmates had known her better. Maarten Oosthuizen had known her from choir. The database had Maarten living in Outerkerk. He'd teased Gerrit sometimes, calling him Anneke's secret boyfriend, but mostly Maarten's attention had been consumed by football and footballers (why hadn't Gerrit been able to sum Maarten up that neatly at the time?). He sat a little taller and typed: Just seeing what old classmates are up to.

Meike padded back into the kitchen, barefoot, in pajamas.

"What are you writing?" she said.

"An email. An old classmate."

"Didn't I tell you? Now you'll want to find everyone."

Gerrit held his fingers a few centimeters above the keyboard. Maarten might already be reading the email, might be replying. But the next morning, Gerrit had only the usual names in his inbox: Meike, a few government ministers, bank officials. Rain blurred his office window. Then an email from Maarten, apologizing for its delay: I was coming in from Singapore. Maarten was a pilot for KLM. He would be in Rotterdam for forty-eight hours. If Gerrit could put up with him groggy and punchy, they should get together. Maarten mentioned no partner. Gerrit replied: You'll have to meet my girlfriend.

Definitely, Maarten emailed back.

"Does he like Indian?" Meike said on the phone at lunch. "I passed a new take-away place." She was so good-natured. But then, she loved showing off their flat. That was the joy of being in your thirties: things to point to and say *mine*.

Gerrit opened wine at the kitchen counter while Meike unwrapped the naan bread and samosas. Maarten sat at the table, his cologne needling past the curry and into Gerrit's nose like cedar.

"I didn't know wine went with Indian food," Maarten said.

"You know you're only here to tell me Gerrit's secrets." Meike slid her hand down the seat of Gerrit's pants.

"Did Gerrit have secrets?" Maarten said. "Well—Anneke."

"Not me." Gerrit swirled his wine glass under his nose.

"You were always poking her," Maarten said. "You can only tease a girl like that if you're gay or dating."

"Gerrit never pokes me," Meike said.

"Maybe you need to ask him," Maarten said.

"And you?" Gerrit said. "You must be seeing someone."

"My job is not so good for relationships," Maarten said. "I wanted to be a fighter pilot, but, you know: the Netherlands. Both our jets have pilots already."

All through dinner, Gerrit watched him and Meike, how at home they seemed together. But then Meike was at home with anyone. Maarten had turned out handsome, with a strong jaw and almost shaved head. He'd kept his agile football movements, shifting in his chair, swiveling, leaning forward and back.

"Aren't you surprised none of us found one another sooner?" he said.

Indeed, the thirty-three students in their class at The Hague International School had seemed like a large ensemble cast, even when Gerrit had felt his only place was backstage.

"I admit, I wouldn't have picked you for the one to find me," Maarten said. "I've been out of touch with everyone. Almost everyone." He looked for classmates in the corners. "How'd you get my address, anyway?"

"It's my fault," Meike said.

"Naturally," Maarten said.

"Why naturally?" Meike bit her lower lip, the way she did waiting for Gerrit's punch lines.

"I'm going to find everyone in our class," Gerrit said. "I am."

After they bid Maarten goodnight he logged back onto the pension database. He found email addresses for all but two of his Dutch classmates. Could there be a more innocuous misuse of a government resource? On the social utility, he found nine of the foreigners. The emails were easy to write, and if enough people replied, what he was writing would be true: I'm putting together a class reunion, online, and if we want, in person. Sitting in bed after Meike had turned out her light, as he typed he saw each person going about his or her tiny, distant business, unaware of being in the past: Claire with her hand-rolled cigarettes, Jan with his Vespa, Wouter with his red pants and (reportedly) excellent weed, Sonja in slim black slacks and turtleneck and black frame glasses, planning to become an architect. Typing Anneke's name, Gerrit saw Katarina laugh at herself for being late to lunch, and everyone at the table sliding aside for her to sit.

That would have been in the few weeks when Gerrit had dared to join her friends at lunch, after the play, before Christmas. After that Katarina and Anneke's father was posted to the United Nations and Katarina and Anneke moved to New York. Their mother was American. That had been nothing to remark on until they left. Everyone at school could speak English; Katarina's had just been more nasal. A different accent than Anneke's, now that Gerrit thought of it.

In his remaining years there, neither had written, to him or, as far as he knew, to anyone else. It would have been harder then, before email. Airmail stamps; that thin blue paper. He wondered if Katarina had stayed in New York. For a while, at university, he'd thought how he would have no trouble getting hired at a New York bank. Americans thought British-sounding English was sexy.

Wouter's was the first reply. He was a sound engineer in London. Gerrit might have heard his latest UK single on Top of the Pops? Claire was a EU agriculture minister. Jan mentioned no work, just a townhouse on a canal in Amsterdam.

"Why is that so special?" Meike had the duvet pulled up around her for the night.

"It makes me sound boring," Gerrit said.

"So, don't be boring."

Gerrit stood beside the bed, hands clasped behind his back.

"Let's talk about long term yield and short term bonds," he said.

The next day he had an email from Sonja—you knew it, an architect, building apartment towers in Dubai. Predictable! She was the twenty-fourth to reply. And Gerrit had gone eighteen years without missing these people! Seeing them all in his inbox, and looking out his office window, he saw Rotterdam as a dot on a room-sized military map, little flags marking New York, London, Singapore, and white strings connecting the flags to him.

One Wednesday Gerrit and Meike woke late. They'd been waking at the same time lately, every morning facing into the sun, Meike leaning into him, his left arm comfortably under her pillow, his right leg over hers, a position they'd found while sleeping. The night before she'd bitten his nipples and, the last he remembered, he'd decided she was hinting and bent down, shyly bulky, nosing closed-lipped under her chin, down the warm rise and fall of her chest.

He switched off the alarm. Meike rolled to face him and pushed him down gently onto his back. The blinds above the headboard were open, the window cranked slightly out. She sat up into the sun, blinking, smiling, and pulled off the tee she'd slept in. On the elevated motorway, less than a hundred meters away, tires sped through last night's rain. Meike inched her waist even with Gerrit's, her mouth peering upturned from beneath her hair, and he wondered how many motorists were turning from their way to work and seeing the black-haired girl. She was so deft. Katarina would have had to flip her hair out of Gerrit's face. Her thick, golden hair.

"The drivers can see you," he said.

"Mmm." Meike lowered herself onto him and leaned forward into shadow, chin to his. Usually she was at best patient in the morning, apologetic that she never felt cleaned up enough for work. She knew it was silly. "You're not silly," Gerrit had said. It was her nerves, she'd said. Thinking about her clients. Not him.

"So." He stroked her cheek with his middle finger. "What's new?"

"When do I meet your people?" she said.

"Soon. Was this OK?"

"It was fine." She kissed him. "Don't worry."

In the bath, he let water run down his face into the day to come. He smelled his hands. When he and Meike had gotten together, she was the one more experienced, with men and women. Maybe now she was just being kind. Drying off, he flexed his arms. Funny Gerrit. He would have to join a fitness club. Really, when he compared himself to his classmates or her co-workers, it was astounding she was with him.

The path he bicycled to work curved through red tulips and white and yellow daffodils along the canal, past apartment blocks identical to Meike and Gerrit's. A girl in a red flowered skirt was riding ahead of him, weaving from side to side, dipping her head towards the flowers. The day was going to be warm, the first real day of spring. At the office, he swung his window open. Seawater slapped against the docks. Wind rattled down the side of the building. Even here, the air had a wet soil scent. Gerrit had only a few new emails: a note from his department head, advertisements for erectile dysfunction medications, and, first in the list, a few minutes old, sent while he had been locking his bicycle and walking to the elevator, a reply from Anneke.

Windscreens flashed on the Erasmus Bridge. The letters of Anneke's email doubled and reunited. In an office across the street, a cleaning woman had put down her cloth and spray bottle and was using someone's computer.

I have thought of you, too, off and on through the years, Anneke had written. She lived in Utrecht. She had a daughter and a son. She taught elementary school and designed costumes for a local theatre. I would be glad of a chance to see you. She was always asking; in ninth and tenth grade she had passed notes and asked if he was staying after school and wanted to share homework. I'm very busy, he typed, but happy. He wrote that he loved his job. That he had a girlfriend. Alone on one line with no capital letters, he typed and did not undo before sending: how's katarina?

He organized his pens in their mug by height. He had a meeting at ten o'clock. He could have phrased things better. He should have used capitals; all lowercase looked deliberate. The weird thing, glaring through the wet brightness outside and slipping in through his open window, was that he wasn't looking forward to Anneke's answer.

His computer chirped. I guess you wouldn't have heard. Katarina developed breast cancer when she was twenty-seven. That was when it was discovered. By then it was already quite advanced.

Twenty-seven. Gerrit would have been twenty-six. He could have taken leave from work to care for her. He could have worked double shifts to get her to the best clinics. All this could have happened before Meike.

Except none of it would have. He would never have dared to ask Katarina out. He wouldn't have dared to ask Meike out, if she hadn't first asked for help setting up her computer.

Well, he'd dared now.

Anneke had typed two line breaks. I didn't know you knew her.

Gerrit typed: I didn't, really.

Return.

Return.

So many condoling phrases were available: I'm so sorry to hear about your loss; that's terrible; I wish that I could have done something. Any would have been true, and could have been written by anyone.

The other members of his department were already trickling into the third floor conference room, around a long recessed-lit table under lichen wallpaper. Disbursement procedures were being updated; the department head was sure they would all welcome the simplified paperwork. Gerrit excused himself to the kitchenette across the hall for coffee. An analyst from another department followed, a tall woman with deep red hair. Usually she wore it down around low-cut necklines and Gerrit was too ashamed of his glances to say hello. Today she had it knotted up around chopsticks.

"Aren't you excited?" she said.

"I can hardly stand it," he said.

"This changes everything."

If he explained about Katarina, the analyst would

have the same response as anyone. You don't expect it, so young. He fled with a smile and his coffee, pressing the elevator button until the doors opened and he could pitch himself inside. I wish that I could have done something. Beep—fifth floor—beep—beep. Seven. I can picture twenty years ago as clearly as yesterday. His computer screen was dim against the sky. He reread Anneke's letter. I didn't know you knew her.

He deleted his earlier words. I knew her a little from theatre, not like I knew you, but she always seemed very nice. I'm sure you've already heard everything I could say too many times. I wouldn't have asked if I'd known what you would have to write. I'm so sorry. And he was.

He ate lunch at his desk, crumbling his sandwich on his tongue. Cars crawled on the bridge. He could even identify some of their makes. Everything had its true colors. A derrick was forking freight containers from a ship. He would have to do something really special for Meike that night. He would have to tell her. But first, they would pick up where they'd stopped in the morning. Meike would notice how delicately Gerrit attended to her, only her, in the moments she surrounded him.

"This has changed me," he said aloud. His voice sounded thin and scraped. When Meike called, it cracked.

"Maarten called, after you left for work," she said. "We must have talked for twenty minutes. Just think—if it weren't for me, I never would have met him."

"I'm sorry," Gerrit said. "A lot happened this morning."

"I hope you don't mind," Meike said. "I invited him to dinner."

"Tonight?" Gerrit said.

"You didn't mention any plans."

"It's fine."

"I felt badly. He'd flown all that way from Singapore and I fed him take-away."

Meike's were the kind of plans you could tell people about. Gerrit's plans would have become something else than what he'd wanted, if he'd said them.

He shouldn't have had to plan. And, as always, he was too late.

He stopped at a wine shop on his way home and crossed the tram tracks to the path between the brick walls of back gardens to the canal. The houses and tiled roofs had taken on a sunset orange. Let's get married, he would say, after Maarten had gone. This summer. This May, in the tulips at Keukenhof. Maybe, after years he and Meike had yet to share—with children, though she'd rarely mentioned them—he would be able to tell her. "There was a girl I knew in school," he would begin, casting the story safely before they'd met, and as he continued it would be clear he'd put aside old images, and learned.

He locked his bicycle and took the stairs two at a time. Forgoing the elevator felt good. His calf muscles pulled and yet he felt exempt, as if his body could be shed like clothing. The wine bag swung and crinkled from his hand; the bottles dully clinked. Meike's laughter and Maarten's voice bounced down the white-tiled stairwell.

"Honey, I don't need to know that," Maarten was saying.

Gerrit rested the wine bottles on the landing by

his door and inched two fingers into his pocket towards the key. Then instead, he smoothed his shirt and pants, grinned his eyes into slits, and rang the doorbell.

"Sometimes twice a night," Meike was saying inside.

She swung the door wide. Maarten was standing by the kitchen table, wine glass in one hand, arm around a taller, balder Wouter. Black pants, not red. Four small bags of weed were on the table.

"She made us wait." Wouter fingered one of the bags.

"That was sweet," Gerrit said. Of course, Meike wouldn't have told them he wasn't into weed. She took his hand and pointed his mouth to hers.

"No," she said. "You're sweet."

He pressed her close. Her breasts rose and fell against his chest.

Something was different; how tightly she let him press? Her shape itself? Her perfume, light and thick as pollen? Was there something she hadn't told him? Or that he'd never noticed?

"We've been hearing all about you," Wouter said.

"How's Anneke?" Maarten said.

"Fine." Gerrit slid his hands down the nubs and indentations of Meike's shoulders. Only he knew. "I have good news and bad news."

He brushed Meike's hair from her face.

"So, what have you been telling them?" he said.

He had no idea what she would say.

NATE LIEDERBACH
Werewolves
Romance Unspeculated
Ancestry

WEREWOLVES

Werewolves the size of pepper shakers, shedding like mad, attack the family reunion. Grandpa sees their approach but dentures (+ cataracts?) prevent the sounding of alarm. Subsequently, the cousins' new puppy is engulfed (upon cursory examination the fur did seem a lighter gray): so one slight oversight determining the entire afternoon. Other hints of invasion include a needling in Auntie's throat (though posterity prohibits coughing/clawing); and the punch is unexpectedly diluted; and the deviled eggs now crusted and inert, also, something tastes floury—here the barometer tumbles.

All the while, wrapped in the sweat of crunchy fried chicken, a charming niece, having recently arrived from Spain, long hands tan as black walnut, tan but twice as smooth, feels a fever on the rise and an itching in her tights; this is in one corner. In the other, the true epicenter of reunion, Father sits with his sisters. They're drunk by a crisping fire but at once feel their heads urged forward. It's phantom and compulsory, a light collision of hairlines and a murmur of strange nuance. Everyone smells wet fur and simultaneously imagines their deceased mother—of course she's here with us.

Or it's the miniature werewolves. It's the miniature werewolves, tails disproportionately long, pink glands whistling in then out. But does it matter, because who will remember this day? The rugs will be dry-cleaned, the bottles recycled. Grandpa sells the cottage far below asking price. Overhead, a sad line of last geese and then when spring scrapes back there're paw prints. Far too large. Maybe a cocker spaniel? Or a Portuguese water dog? They lead around the veranda and off toward the shore. A clump of feathers, a pinch of aluminum foil. Hours fall backwards, dragged off like a howl.

ROMANCE UNSPECULATED

His name is Bear. Because of his neck. Or how that earth-stolen beard swallows shadows, glints rich brown off bleachers, throws light into the corners of press rooms. Maybe he's a journalist. Though someone's certain he's a brother to the referee. All that's really known is his sudden afternoon glory. How the umpire is strap-trapped in the sparking circuits of his lofty wheelchair. It lurches and bucks about the court, snorts and barrels for the net. Bear's in its path, but she's not watching. Drops her racket. Pictures balls shooting from her womb like a serving machine. It's a nice day. The machine's nearly empty. This is her story, what's internalized. Three balls left, maybe one. But the real story for the papers seems she's been abstaining. It's in the name of the game. Twenty-seven years and now ripe to retire. Two Grand Slam Cups and a world ranking of #6. In the magazines, below a billowing Vera Wang, the captions read Pillar of Sugar and What a Beard!

After: Portobello bisque, gin gimlets, bacon-wrapped dates stuffed with chevre and smokehouse almonds. Rob Base floods the parquetted lawn. A third cousin, twelve, dry humps the bridesmaids. Serena shows up, doesn't say anything, leaves. The bill's been settled anonymously. Respective kin drive drunkenly off. The couple's alone at some mountain lodge. Under wavering hearth shadows, amidst the sharp casting dance of endangered antlers, his chest: fucking massive. Pressed there, her ear. How it absorbs the call of his strong diaphragm and how he grips her slight waist whilst imagining possibilities of a top-spin slice. The sea can be smelled in the near distance, or just beyond her lycheed hair. A dismayed and stupefied moon bumps those big panes of glass. His only challenger? He laughs the laugh of the Tall Dark Man. He whispers, You just try and come down here, Cheesedick.

The moon shivers, slinks beyond the window frame.

But whoa, dust.

Dust, so much dust—it's what the last lovers had thought (they left without paying). Ha. Bear's prepared for the tiniest of rivals. Tepid tongues prod Claritin into the other's throat. Histamines stymied, these lust-birds have carnality to squander. Piles and folds. Slopes and handfuls. On a kingsize plank with whalebone duvet, but something reminds her of mash potatoes and something reminds him of a lukewarm spa. She says, Let's try this, and reveals a butter knife. With the other hand, a Zippo. She says, Sterilized. Sheepishly, he says, I was thinking Fruit Roll-Up, not tambourine.

Letting the A/C song talk them through an awkward settling down. Finally, arm behind his head, she confides: her twin brother died in a German occupation of post-gay Paris. This clues the husband, yes it fixes everything—quarter-century cherry so calloused, but alas it's no religiosity. Ah-ha, she's a time traveler!

With such possibility his re-arousal's instantaneous. An adventurous energy echoes in the ceiling fan. Rolling onto her knees, she offers sweetly birth-marked buttocks, shouts, "Love-Love!" With a war-cry, he enters. She evaporates.

Disappointing. Certainly. But it's a development within his scope. Hold up a sec, what's this? Part of her hair, scalp, snagged on the headboard. Sweat-matted and green tea conditioned. With such slippery skin and tear-soaked fingers, freeing it's a slow go. And now where to storage our fleshy keepsake? Turning circles, snowshoes on the wall, paintings of aspen. By the leaky door, his boots, tips together, conspire. His eyes fall into them, fill them with humanity: this is the extent of Bear's tragedy, an unshared pathos of crinkled leather, lop-worn heels, split-mouth soles whispering, It's virginity's warm fight to the light and how it never just vanishes but only clouds out. Your pathway, hero, begins at this lodge, but it will be wrought with cracks like years and you won't remember your name…

She, though, does. She remembers his name. Or is it still remembering if it's thirty years before and twenty-three feet below? She's back again, yes. The sound of his footfalls through the wires of root, shivering layers of dirt. The glory of her last life the catastrophe of this. Sediment piled on her lashes, ears, ass crack. Only worms wanting more. If only her displacement would trouble the topsoil where he passes. No. He's barely a boy.

ANCESTRY

Selvin the Christmas Elf drove his pretend-dead girlfriend to Arizona in no direction but two high beams bouncing maybe south over buckled highway to a place where cliffs go to die, where cliffs drag themselves like the worms of Dune, across rock seas and deaf clay, thirsting, he imagined, for newness, for lush grass, for supreme flatness, but finding only heaps of ancestry, so that first night he slept with her body in the truck bed and the huskies curled on their shins while an autumn storm converged from Baja to ping the camper shell and whistle the window slits to where at one point a gust jiggled the axels and he thought his pretend-dead girlfriend had moved—unnerving—but then in the reality of morning, Selvin the Christmas Elf made a fire from wet cardboard as ravens circled like cursed Girl Scouts and he burned everything he could find, a new world of vibrating floors of smoke until, waking with a loose cough, pretend-dead girlfriend slinked over the tailgate, took up a plastic spoon, fed them pre-stirred yogurt, and soon they'd stripped off their road-spiced, North Pole uniforms to fuck graciously on the rain-beaded truck hood (even though, way before ejaculation, Selvin the Christmas Elf, still stuck in that long-gone crevasse, scowled at the huskies for all the fruitlessness of their mock battles, thinking, It's all just play, and Is that why I left?) but now the haze was clearing, beyond the girl's sharpened ears, a muddled sun that reminded him to concentrate on scraping, not violently, but steadily, cock like a crooked finger, the worker who works for wonder alone—or no, the man with the plan, the one who escaped, who couldn't rectify revolution and individuation, who saw through the lies but couldn't do it alone, had to drag her into it, just like now: he's done, yanked loose, condom cast on the last smoldering log, all noxious smoke but no chimney, no plate of cookies, nothing to keep it ordered.

NOTES FROM A BURNING UNDERGROUND
Jonathan Callahan

Let me explain.

"Let" being of course superfluous here, where I am God, but infinitely appropriate in the presence of Truck, to whom I intended to deliver my treatise in toto, only one needed permission to address Professor Truck, Professor Truck's rhetorical posture was that of a hilltop castle, an immense castle, absolutely impregnable, a fortress defended by ramparts and bulwarks, dimwitted men in chain mail willing to die en masse at a word from their lord, so that one entertained the mere prospect of approach with foreboding, a shift of the lip was all Truck would need to evince his professional distaste for my methods, so that rather than risk being embarrassed again, I often eschewed expression altogether, though I had many things to say, in silence allowed Truck to carry on with his nonsense while I improved upon a number of clever schemes to dispense with the gloating man's life. But that day, on the hardwood, adrenaline made me unusually brave.

Let me explain, I repeated, I grunted, as he posted me up. But he wouldn't.

Executing an ungainly reverse pivot—an inarguable travel I didn't dare call—Truck loped into the lane, lofted a hideous hook-shot high over my head that improbably—but inevitably—swooped through the net without touching rim. Twenty-one he said, smiling. I had eight.

Truck and I had commenced our supposed friendship by chance, at a karaoke bar just off-campus, where a small contingent of Humanities faculty had convened for a mixer conjured by our provost to facilitate bonhomie. In that sultry singing hall a grinning Professor T (he was often grinning) approached me as I toweled perspiration from my neck to express his admiration for my vigorous rendition of a certain unjustly neglected gem I'd reclaimed from the coffers of late-century hip-hop. "Nasty," he laughed, suspending a closed fist for me to bump with one of my own. I was once an excellent rapper. In point of fact, I know quite a bit about rap, much more than most professional rappers know: genealogies, sources, aesthetic trends; it was even once my habit to extemporize bursts of bravura freestyle verse but who would believe me if I were to assert as much now?

Soon we were taking our meals together, in the student-faculty dining hall—a dismal establishment staffed by cheerless Hispanics with limited lexicons, poor compensation, absurdly long hours and in general scant inducement not to defile an ala carte item demanded sans "please." Over charred burgers and fried mozzarella Truck loved to regale me with yarns of ivory hijinks and professorial jest: the preposterous students; our peers' reams of feeble investigations, published in quarterlies perused, mainly, by the contributing parties themselves: department heads, alumnae, chairpersons, deans, other figures of administrative sway dealt department-lounge pleasantry and cocktail-greased praise, the odd besotted co-ed whisked decorously to bed, later gently nudged along with a few months of future memoir–material and an inflated grade at an enjoyable semester's end. I chewed, and appraised long passing legs, waiting for gaps in his discourse for the chance to preface remarks I would have liked to contribute to our between-class repasts. But there were no such gaps.

I usually tried to look pensive as Truck urged me to perceive the cutthroat sterility beneath every guffaw, every crass in-class aside snuck by our dumb students, or lobbed over their heads, every earthy backslap exchanged between ostensible brethren in letters who secretly found their colleagues insipid beyond contempt. Isn't this—here he might gesture theatrically at whichever thick volume lay bristling with neon micro-Post-Its beside his plastic lunch tray—what we've decided to do with ourselves? Aren't we supposed to be the good guys?

We flipped in a few post-contest lay-ups. I moved out to the arc. Truck tried, not for the first time, to explain that I might significantly increase my shooting percentage by snapping my wrist forward and following through. Meanwhile, on defense I was frequently flat in the foot, thus surrendering what he claimed was my best counter to his considerable height advantage, my speed, though in fact I have never been fast.

"What are you writing these days, Truck?" I wondered.

As a young man not yet out of grad school he'd published his polemic, a raging denunciation of more or less everyone, but specifically taking to task two groups of citizens: the post-internet generation just then coming of age, a roaring disappointment to Truck, these youth—who, yes, of course had been battered since birth by the robust exertions of multinational commerce, forces too perniciously large for most folks to detect, let alone resist, legitimately hoodwinked into massive passivity, yes, but who also didn't really seem to mind. "Relax, Bro," he titled his book's first half.

But it was for the next group that Professor Truck reserved the special wrath of his book's second half, a blistering sparsely-punctuated screed excoriating academics. Who, Truck argued, having done the interminable headwork, annotated pages deep into countless CNS-enhanced nights, sat through seminars, read untold books and journals, ground out dissertations—who were in other words perhaps cognitively equipped for the battle being waged behind most of the oblivious population's back and might constitute the last viable counterforce to Capital's inexorable tread. The pencil heads might be heroes! he claimed—but instead they'd lost themselves in their labyrinths of personal expertise, in their arcane argot, their inaccessible bullshit, insider back-and-forth ("credence-jostling," as he called it). Truck, on the other hand was for a scholarship that meant something to somebody not wearing tweed (not that many of us wore tweed—this was Truck's choice of phrase). Truck was for a scholarship that saves lives.

Naturally, *The Malaise that Thickens Unto Death* housed no original claims. (As the near-two-million-and-counting copies sold [factoring in not insignificant sales overseas] ought to prove.) However, it was a sensation. He parlayed his triumph into a lucrative stint at S——— College, where we both found ourselves among the younger members of the faculty team. On accepting his post, Truck was already well known, a celebrity, not only around campus, but wherever he went, more or less. My own work was not known outside of scholarly circles.

"Almost done with Dis: Illusion," he said, "after that, well, who can tell?"

Truck opposed all illusions. He was out to demolish hypocrisy, once and for all. Nothing got him off like giving it to the odd department head, or using his platform to remind the rogue campus poet that despite all her spleen she was still securely ensconced in her hated high-middle class.

"Truck," I told him, "Truck: you're kind of an asshole. You're a complete asshole. Anyone ever tell you that? How old are you?"

"You're just saying that. Thirty-one."

"Death coming soon."

"Think so?"

"You've wobbled over the peak. Never even felt it happen. Soon you'll be picking up downward speed. Think about that reverse I snuck past you."

"Well."

"Getting old."

"You pushed off with your left hand. Blatant foul. I didn't call it because what was the point?"

"Death scoping out property in your code."

"Death not necessarily knocking, but maybe hanging out at the end of the drive, you're saying."

"You see Death sprinting under a scythe-shaped kite in the field at the end of your block."

"Deathgrams encrypted in the dentist's bills. You're older than I am, ass."

"Death not as distant these days. Death closing in."

Death, yes: but murder? If I were to kill Henry L. Winston Truck how many Trucks might rise up in his place? A Truck at the corner of every street. I could devote a life to extermination and never rid a single town of its Trucks. Then too, I didn't necessarily even want to kill every Truck. This Truck, sometimes, yes, but not every iteration of Truck. I wanted to move these men, shape them, somehow eradicate the Truckness without destroying the Truck. My *assassination drive*, as I took to tagging it in journals logged during this time, was accordingly a form of capitulation: I wanted to kill what I lacked the power to touch. And what was it I wanted to touch? Killing Truck would solve nothing. (Or little.) For every Truck slaughtered I'd still be surrounded by uncountable Trucks.

On the other hand, Truck kept becoming less possible to stand.

Blithe Truck casing the warrens of Humanities halls, pausing to pummel some student with volleys of casually discharged argot, because he could. His epistemes and ecriture, allusive esotera, the names, the scholarship, nomenclature braided into easy conversation about MTV and Empire, Internet commerce and Death—synchrony, illocution, misprision, Lebenswelt! he shouted, from the coffee lounge, Einfühlung, the irony so densely layered on that one struggled to sort out the targets from targeteers. That very evening he'd be back in a packed auditorium, up to his usual saving of lives. But whose life was he out to save?

Our weekly one-on-one hoops sessions were an unrelenting shame. Tall Truck routinely swatted my lay-up attempts off the glass, calling fouls on himself when he'd cleanly caught my shot (meanwhile refusing to acknowledge his persistent and blatant reliance on the illegal hand check). Only an analogous pounding on the college's clay tennis courts would have been more personally painful, as we may or may not subsequently see, depending on how soon I decide to burn these notes.

I lived in a small second-floor apartment off campus. I had very few other friends. The only furnishings of note were a bookshelf, a bed, a framed photograph of my mother on a table of varnished black wood, and (in replica) the bones of a man who'd stood nearly seven feet tall. One night, as I sat weeping, awash in cheap gin, at the foot of the gnomic illustration I seemed to have Sharpied onto my wall—an admittedly crude rendition of the primal scene—I gave in to a vision of redemption and glory. Somehow, one day my idea would rise from these dissipate ashes like a great golden bird, or maybe a monolith, a towering effigy of the man I'd always wanted to be, the man it hurt not to be, this man, alive now, arisen, striding forth at dawn, shadow casing the territory before him as he nears the mist-wreathed city thrust up over cracked earth, a black Stetson's brim pulled low over his brow, this drifter, this calm boss of the plains, shrouded in black, as well as in mystery, loping toward his destiny, at last prepared to stare into the eyes of men—only I didn't have a vision of any me other than what I was not.

Picture the harried humanities professor from your undergraduate days. You remember? A man who, it's palpable, from his youth must have loved learning. One imagines him snug on some ottoman through the long afternoons, indifferent to sunlight and kid-whoops streaking in from outside as he soaks in the stories of famines and plagues, intrigue, calamity, war, peace, survival, progress, relapse, culture, barbarity, life, death, struggle and hope, a book-loving boy, not necessarily intelligent or even wise, an indifferent sportsman, not what his father might call "handy," destined, in short, to haunt lecture halls and libraries in the hopes of attaining an associate-professorship, and tenure, should he make it that far.

In his lectures, ever-frantic to unburden himself, the poor man pontificates, more allegro appassionato as the hour wanes . . . the hour's end nears, his young charges squirm, writing implements perform increasingly acrobatic feats over platforms of knuckle and thumb, mutters, embellished coughs, yawns, somebody's phone goes off, the clock's hands resist a collective extra-sensory admonishment to move . . . see how our hero streaks toward the terrible moment when the first student with guts will decide Enough, later, asshole, baseball cap (worn inside in direct violation of undergraduate handbook) shading face, and now it's only backs, an exodus ascends the aisles between stadium seats, files for various exits, perhaps to reconvene for a greasy snack, or some hackey-sack out in the quad, or maybe to trot under those famed florescent spinning discs—Frisbees. These mutineers clatter from amphitheatrical seats, begin to disperse, even as a fearsome apodosis heaves into view, prepares to shake the inner chambers of what in quainter times was called the soul, a thundering finale to which the lecturer's whole preceding hour-and-a-half has been but a prelude, the breath of life that these early leave-takers won't hear and wouldn't understand if they did, since their attention has been flagging for some time, perhaps even for the entire time, on a morning when many are still not quite recovered from last night's Dioneysian fun—What's this joker's point, Bro? Which part do we need to know for the test?

On the other hand I have secretly sat in on any number of Truck's lectures—in inventive disguise: false mutton chops, capacious jeans, and, at first, a baseball cap of my own until the near-calamitous morning Truck demanded mid-lecture in front of my several-hundred fellow lecturees that I remove my headwear indoors as demanded by handbook law, so that I was forced to flee the cavernous hall, barely dodging a burly enthusiast near the back who attempted to intervene on his professor's behalf (the only session I missed that semester of the entire insipid series)—seen all pens ascribble till the moment he steps back from the rostrum and bows, to emotion-rich applause.

Have I pointed out I'd compiled any number of infinitely superior theses, dissertations, treatises, bits of metaphysical speculation, thought experiments, logical proofs, cultural dissections, arguments toward a new socio-economic world order in lieu of the ruling neoliberal capitalist regime, sonnets in all the traditional forms (with an especial emphasis on the rhyme scheme of the Bard), prose poems, light verse, film scripts, film critiques, villanelles, volumes of critical discourse, meditations, labyrinths, philosophical dialogues, disquisitions, an uncompleted epic poem in cantos waltzing from Gaelic to Hindi to Latin to Greek (my Italian not yet up to the task), a rock opera, several symphonies the college orchestra declined to perform, as well as various other trifles in my notes? I had. However: Truck had a finger on the popular heartbeat, Truck had the vast vapidity of the culture by the throat, and in this sense (and in this sense alone) was neither charlatan, nor phoney, nor hack, but pure product of his times, that clown, a reality only I had the lucidity to see, let alone find distressingly bleak.

Truck put his arm around my shoulder, suggested we head for the showers. He enjoyed showering in the unstalled locker room for obvious reasons. Something split in me. His hand was on my shoulder, his breath was in my ear, I looked up and embarked on a thorough description of what I would do to him one day, the methodical approach I would take to dismantling his corporeal vessel, time permitting, since my whole life has been one long race against self-inflicted death, and I couldn't guarantee the fate I articulated in meticulous detail as he slowly eased his hold on my shoulder and backed away, mouth agape, but I assured him I would do all I could do to ensure it was his.

"Everything in my power!"

I bellowed a choice bit of untranslatable Japanese, leapt up onto a wall-mounted bench and banged my fist against the nearest locker's thin steel.

Truck called for help.

"I'll assemble an arsenal," I enthused, "of implements designed to inflict maximum pain!"

"Stop this." He was shaking his head as if he believed in so doing he might negate me.

"Change of plan," I decided: "I'll eat you alive!"

He whinnied and dashed round a locker-bank for the door as I bounded down from my perch, grunting with hatred and joy.

Of course a star cornerback with sea gaskets for triceps and a yeoman's love for his famous old prof was waiting in a half-crouch to intervene, pinning me to the foot-fragrant Berber wall-to-wall while I squirmed and heaved.

"Everything in my power," I breathed.

Of course "everything in my power," is a signifying phrase that lacks a clear referent when applied to a powerless man. The provost declined the reasonable alternative I proposed to his offer of granting indefinite psychiatric leave: that we subject Truck's so-called treatise to review by a panel of reputable or even competent scholars I offered to personally handpick. I was left with little choice but to cite my disenchantment with the utter lack of intellectual integrity displayed by an ostensibly well-regarded academic institution—"You're only in it for the money," I barely had the energy to note—and, barring reconsideration of my proposed compromise, resign my post, a post I reminded the provost he was hardly likely to fill with a candidate my equal in acuity, rigor, generosity, expertise, to say nothing of raw skill, so that it was not a personal affront or slap in my face when this resignation was accepted so much as it was a debasing of an entire department, an irreparable marring of an until then widely admired school of arts and letters, a fact I reiterated more than once and in not unheated tones as I strode through the door, kicking over a stack of books on my way out.

Exterminate

the

Excuse me.

Of course, I had it all wrong—later on, during those first awful months after I relinquished my position on the faculty of the distinguished liberal arts college which good taste forbids me to cite here by name, I took a job waiting tables at a small bar and grill, a national chain, recently the beneficiary of a successful rebranding campaign, a series of television spots by a fat Food Network figurehead. Only one employee had even heard of Truck—and she copped to having never read his work! One night I accepted my employee-perk half-price on a plate of insipid potatoes, then left. At the screen door, on apprehending the import of my suitcases and bags, my bleary-eyed mother looked sad, but not necessarily surprised.

In the beginning, as I lay groaning on the uncomfortable cot in the basement beneath groaning floorboards (my mother's subtle footfalls the predawn antipode to the restless pacing of my insomniac brain), I'd often catch myself peering further into my piteous past, trying to extract something like sense, a reason, a thread; or compiling lists of all the things I'd ever loved: Reasons to Live. There were few. Mostly what I thought of were things I didn't even like. And if you can't conjure a modest list of lovable features of life, how are you supposed to summon what needs summoning to ride out everything else? Why should you?

"Got it, Buddha," a female buddy'd once quipped, when I tried to explain my inability to get up the will to do what was expected of me when I knew in the end I'd be dust, and until then, profoundly unhappy. This was when we were students ourselves. I'd decided to take a degree in kinesiology, as a sort of penance for my failed tennis career—which is to say I was studying to become a P.E. teacher.

We were at a bar, or outside a bar, out back, in a cool September breeze, me smoking a cigarette, her holding her lager or ale, half-pint sloshing from side to side in her unsteady hand, casually suggesting that I come on back inside. I declined, not yet having fully articulated my position. Perhaps I should have simply gone. She'd asked me here, she seemed to want to spend some time with me, it was possible that we would fuck. But there, on the veranda of a bar that happened also to be called "The Veranda," as she sat beside me on a little ledge built right into the half-wall of heavy wooden planks, my desire to fuck her was subordinated by my desire to make her see.

With a shrug this well-lubricated half-friend turned to re-enter the bar. Were this the future (that is, now) I might have invited this young woman (who was not unattractive, in her sloe-eyed, docile, way, possessed of a goodnaturedly ignorant charm) to consider several passages I might then quote verbatim—Nietzche, Freud, Goethe, and especially Shakespeare as channeled through Macbeth, that tormented thane—however, having done so, I'd have hastened to add: no quotes were necessary: you needn't crack these dusty tomes, no call for consulting relics if you're willing to think just a bit for yourself. However, this was then; I lacked the will- and firepower I would in mid-adulthood gain. I imagined punching her in the breast. Instead, after chiding her for reluctance to exercise her brain, I heaved into a fresh exposition of my thesis as she peered into her stein.

A second-string halfback paced unsteadily past.

"Ditch the zero, get with a hero," he said.

Stupefyingly, she did join this athletic oaf and his merry band—only later did I learn they'd once co-taken a class—and she left, offering only an apologetic shrug and a whispered suggestion that I find her inside, "Rescue me in a minute or two," as she made her own way back in.

Under a puny moon, I stood with my hands on the veranda's cracked wooden railing and looked out at the makeshift lot crowded with a chaos of all sorts of trucks and cars (I noted in passing what struck me as an atypical proliferation of jeeps) and started to weigh my options. "But isn't that the problem?" I asked myself—literally asked myself, aloud, and not under my breath in a near-whisper or even a subdued mutter but at vocal full-throttle, my inquiry's echo caroming off car hoods and jeep-windshields and up into the night. "Fool!" I shouted, in a moment of thunder "it's ALWAYS the options: never the choice!" I spun and reentered the bar called Veranda. I spotted my friend, whose name, incidentally, was Puff, near the back, and while mouthing the word "Choice" to myself nudged my way to the bar, at some point en route altering my mantra to "Act," which I'd decided was closer to what I meant, and then—as I waited for the bartender to serve other patrons, then some more patrons who'd clearly arrived after me, and then a gang of chattering girls with gilded faces and sculpted coifs, whose baroque requests burdened my overworked mixoloxist for a solid seven minutes, and then an enormous bearded man beside me who wanted a stout and whose proximity left the bartender nearly no choice but to ask me what I needed—"Do," I muttered aloud, "Do" was a definite improvement on "Act"—it could constitute a whole personal philosophy, I felt—"Sorry?" asked the barman, furrowing his lone brow, hand theatrically cupped to ear, face distorted with scowl.

I started to stammer, my mind abruptly an arctic drift unspoiled by the name of a single brew, I couldn't even see the tap over the neon potion–sipping clique's considerable perms, and I hadn't decided what to drink yet, had not weighed my options, and the horror of inadequacy in the eyes of my fellow men, my quintessent lack, reminder of why I preferred even then to drink alone, the internal gulf came roaring open again like a field of empty tennis courts, and I saw the full folly of "Do": of course I can't merely "Do," as other men Do, I'm missing something that enables their Do, I contemplated a tail-tucked flight from the Veranda until a lyric to a song I'd not heard in years bounced into that mental vacuity like a tennis ball dropped from heaven, and though I could have wept with gratitude, I nodded, cool, with narrowed eyes: "One bourbon, one Scotch, one beer."

After an only half-awkward exchange (the bar's selection of Scotch was sizable: I selected an attractive red label at random) I downed my distillates and hefted my pint of headless ale toward the table where Puff and her new drinking partners were swapping banal bits culled from their respective personal histories.

I interposed with a roared "WHAT'S UP?" and greeted Puff with an affectionate pat on the head. My hand, perhaps a bit heavy with liquor, came down harder than intended.

Puff flinched away.

"Ah, what the fuck B———? That hurt!"

From one of several indistinguishable specimens of brawn: "Yeah, what the fuck B———?"

"WHAT'S HAPPENING?" I asked.

After a long pause during which it did not occur to me to feel fear, Puff muttered, "I think you should go home."

THE NIGHT IS YOUNG!"

A second friend said, "Dude, you look like shit."

Here I tried some ineffective riposte to the effect that he was the one who looked like shit, aaaand—

(Standing up): "What's that?"

I revised, managed nothing more potent.

Naturally, things began to swell, I dimly recall pounding my fist on the table, staring hard at a spot just north of one of one football fellows' brow in an imitation of grim eyelock, more insults were bartered, I scoffed at their stupidity, they ridiculed my modest paunch, my slurred words, my lack of what they conceived of as fashion sense (I had on an Atlantic-blue blazer in excellent taste), my choice of major, and soon Puff had started to cry, I suppose seeing what was in the offing, all women are Cassandras, no, that's an exaggeration, but some seem to have a prescience for this sort of thing, as I grimly trailed the young men into the lot out back. We snaked in an almost stately procession through columns of jeeps and cars, arriving at a secluded patch of asphalt, dust, broken glass, where, under a cloud- and mostly moon-less sky, I swung without warning for my enemy's face, missed, took a powerful knee to the groin, stumbled, half-saw the impending faux-leather boot, then a fist clenched around some unsportsmanlike protrusive gleamings, and then

"Here, the big cut is bleeding again," Puff said, with one hand proffering a fresh napkin extracted from her purse while with the other she navigated a leftward turn through an empty intersection.

"Again?" I asked.

"Those fucking assholes."

Leering out at me from the small rectangle of mirror ensconced in the felt flap folded down over the windshield's upper rim was a grotesque caricature of an injured young man who vaguely resembled myself: vampirically sallow, one eyelid fixed at half-mast, several disgusting gashes criss-crossing his temples and cheeks, a rivulet of purple-red blood dripping from his left nostril.

Good Puff took good care of me that night, whisking me away from what, unbeknownst to me, had become the scene of a crime. In desperation I'd flailed for my mauling attacker's face while he knelt and methodically mashed up my own, that unsporting clutched or worn metal improving on his already-effective bare fists. He'd shrieked and reeled back, blood dripping from a hand cupped over one eye, smashed his gloved fist through a neighboring car's window, car alarms sounding as witnesses came pouring out of The Veranda, sparing me who knows what further consequence, as the footballers took off in a battered Ford truck.

I was in bad shape indeed, until Puff reappeared in her sleek sedan and assisted me into the passenger seat (I remember none of this, though I was apparently able to hobble) and we made our escape.

But I was ungrateful. I howled with fury and shame, demanded that she let me out so that I could "hunt the fucks down," but she would not. I insulted her. I told her my reconfigured face was her fault. She begged me to calm down; I refused, spewing insults, calling her terrible things. I told her she was unattractive and getting a bit fat. I told her I wouldn't have bothered to help her in reversed circumstances (which was true). In the end, she deposited me at my on-campus apartment, where a roommate of mine she'd called to awaken perturbedly waited to assist me to bed, and, as her little sedan eased off into the night, I perceived that I'd spent my last evening in the company of Puff.

I vowed to return to the Veranda every night for the next several weeks, or as long as it took, until I could find my enemies and, removing the sunglasses and surgeon's mask I wore to conceal the spectacular inscriptions they'd left on my face, challenge them to a duel. I didn't know precisely what sort of duel (my father had fenced, a common decadence among a certain strain of military men, but he'd never taught me) but after they failed to appear on either of the next two evenings I took to pacing the streets of our shabby little college town's "downtown," a long lane of interchangeable bars, in the vain half-hopes of our paths intersecting and my exacting bloody recompense for that very bad evening, but I was never to see them again—a relief, naturally, though one I was too ashamed to admit that I felt.

But eventually I did admit it. Toe to toe with these behemoths I couldn't conceivably win. I had to find a way to slip past the stupidity—or, to lift lingo from the barbarians' own horde, execute an end-around, or again, to put it in terms taken from the annals of American folk wisdom: one day I wanted them to be pumping my gas. I dreamed of a life that wouldn't come down to who could muscle whom out of position. I thought: There must be some other way to live. Naturally Nietzsche would disagree, but how could I have known that then? I began reading books. Soon I'd embarked on my course of humanitarian self-education, which, as I have adequately demonstrated above, was of course just another mistake.

Reasons to live, reasons to live… well. What about tennis? I had been in early adolescence an avid if mediocre tennis player, and while more often I preferred to sequester myself on the practice courts where I might hone my arsenal of shots by firing them off against the green paint-chipped monster of a wall (or "N.V.", as I privately called it), I would occasionally linger along the fringes of the outdoor courts at our local community center until someone's partner pulled up lame—groin, ankle, knee: I would find myself half hoping for such an injury and the competitive opportunity it would provide while simultaneously dreading the subsequent contest I would thereby be compelled to complete to the point that I'd entertain the idea of pretending to roll my own ankle while jogging over to the other court— and I was invited to compete for a couple of sets. Darting across the practice court, I would envision myself in just such an impromptu contest, gigantic N.V. assuming the role of an immense stalwart opponent possessed of an impeccable if somewhat predictable return game. In a racquetwhirling dream I'd pirouette through the precise tracings of intricate patterns air-etched by my own bodily motion, necessarily never winning a point, but often sustaining the imagined volley for so long that time seemed not merely to stretch but to fray, into a fluffy thing, like the deplasticized tips of the laces tufted through the topmost eyelets of my "lucky" tennis shoes…immaterial …these volleys lasting much longer than any undertaken with sentient partners, my sense of self nearly atomized, all the restrictions of corporeal being seeming to effervesce as the "I" that I believed I must be was diffused across a bodiless state of freefloating grace, or a current flowing in loops like an invisible "8" round the syncopated beating of the tennis ball's "pock"s, and I became something more than myself—or perhaps less: an extract, a distillate of my own ordinarily diluted perfect particles, too crudely and hastily stirred in with the offal and gunk of imperfect experience for anyone else ever to appreciate (or see)… Invariably I would walk from the practice court after one of these sessions hot with triumph, sure that when I next descended upon the community center's courts, the blood-fueled opponent chosen to stand in for impassive N.V. (whose perfection I'd been able to meet, stroke for stroke, almost), would be staggered with awe. Possibly a small-to-medium-sized crowd would gather to witness the match, and they, too, would be awestruck by the skill, the precision, the glory, the power, the beauty, the art of the transient architecture my slicing racquet nimbly carved.

Onlookers did, in fact, frequently gather beside those courts, not strictly to spectate so much as to keep tabs on matches in progress and secure their own position on the court—but watching, nevertheless: so that the losses' humiliation was magnified—when my failure to return even my opponent's most lazily-placed shots began visibly to annoy him (or her) and

I perceived his (or her) frustration over my inability to provoke the expenditure of even token effort, I would furiously redouble my own, will myself to focus a bit harder, lighten my feet, concentrate keep your eye on the fucking ball, B——, only to find the more fiercely I focused, the more difficult it became to make even the most glancing, ineffectual contact with the ball, so that I'd often close a match by failing to connect with five consecutive serves. I'd afterwards grimly shake hands and accept my opponent's dishonest gratitude for the match, inwardly steeling myself against the ludicrous tears on the inevitable brink of gushing forth, pledging to return that night, after dark, for a flagellant extra session on the practice court, with N.V.

We now roar forward through half-remembered time. The subsequent scene finds your narrator still residing at home, meek, though not penitent, having renounced the university for good, the young ex–doctor of the humanities sketching feeble prose poems on the transient stationery of sleep-desperate thought to pass nights in his widowed mother's basement, where his boxed possessions form a sort of fort or parapet around the cot his limbs stick to and probe for some semblance of repose, in vain. What was keeping me up? Well, I still wanted to kill my ex-colleague, of course, but back then it was all I could do to pour milk into my cereal without the weeping and sobs, let alone leave the house, let alone stalk the corridors of S—— College at night, lie in wait for the unsuspecting public intellectual, sneak up from behind with the rag and duct tape, machete, so forth.

Tempting as it may be for the time-traveling autohistorian to seek out specific causes, to guess at the Ur cause that left him no choice but to set out then on the path that one day led to now, it's of course important to consider that there may be none. Might I have been merely mad? True, my father had passed on, leaving me nil—but I'd long expected as much, and the truth was, I hated the prick, and even if his death hadn't been coming for a good half-decade or more, I wouldn't have wept at his wake (which was lugubriously overwrought: folded flags, bugles, canonfire, the like). In the interests of isolating motive, I suppose it'd have been better to see him die violently at the hands of some hateful subhuman, gunned down for a wallet or watchband to be plucked from the lifeless corpse. No such luck. However, I didn't need a singular catastrophe to perceive the sprawling catastrophic tableau. What, do you?

Eventually I found more menial work. Mother begged. But what a miserable employee I was during those miserable months! I could regale you, Reader, with countless tales of humdrum failure, but I'm beginning to wonder who I expect to care about these things. Not that I care whether anyone will care. How could you care or not? I intend to deprive you of the choice, once I've hurled this obscene constipation into the fireplace (I don't have a fireplace; I will find one) or some comparable conflagration, the blaze that will sizzle and crackle, consuming these sentences' sickening, bloat. But not until I've explained it all.

I worked in an office. One morning a supervisor (not my supervisor, just someone I'd often seen strutting the dismal halls of my workplace's small office complex with a supervisory air. I couldn't positively claim he was a supervisor) was passing my desk. I had been shuffling papers from one stack to another for some time so as to sustain an industrious air, but perhaps I'd momentarily let my hands go idle; I looked up to see this particular supervisor. He had just one arm, his name, I believe, was "Wrangler," the purest of pricks, and this particular morning he met my eyes as I happened to look up from my pensive daze, that smile on his ruddy overfed face as he chortled, not slowing his gait, "Must be nice."

I stared after him, not especially worried about my job security, he wasn't *my* supervisor, and anyway I was near enough to the company's bottom rung—actually the position I held most likely constituted the company's bottom rung, regardless of the several-cent raise I'd recently been awarded, presumably for shuffling the papers from one stack to another without getting in anyone's way (I avoided the phones)—as to not merit more than this sort of snide commentary upon my general lack of worth.

"NICE"? I was half-inclined to roar: "NICE? You think you know who I am?"

But of course, he didn't know who I was. Or maybe he knew just enough to know it didn't matter who I was. I didn't matter to anyone. I imagine this will sound trite, sentimental, who knows (or cares—I reiterate my intention to burn these notes), but it was this sudden insight—that is, that in order for this one-armed mid-level office manager and the whole mass of living men for whom I suddenly perceived he must stand in as a sort of three-limbed proxy to know me, I would have either to do something awful—something brutal, chilling, horror-inducing, something too thunderously balance-upsetting to be laughed away in passing by any supervisor with more important things on his mind, I would have to shake the earth—or else I would need to become him.

It seemed too late to become anything worthy in the eyes of other men; but how would someone like me shake the earth? Supposing I were to procure an assault rifle, for instance, carry it in the duffel bag in which I ordinarily bore my gym clothes (though upon reaching the gym I more often than not sat in the locker room for a half-hour before deciding to catch the next train after the one that by sitting in the locker room I had missed, calculating I could use the extra time to work through a few pints at the stationside bar). But, no, the thought was too awful—less because I couldn't bear to have the blood of innocent others on my hands than because I was truly terrified of the prospect of being sent to jail. Rape! Torture! I'd rather be this miserable than worse! Or so I said to myself that morning, as I recommenced shuffling my papers between stacks, at nearly double my usual speed, even going so far as to create a series of new stacks which I then seamlessly incorporated into the procedure in a kind of intricate weave, my face a blank mask of grim focus motivated by this newly-arisen need to be witnessed by the next passing supervisor hard at work until I grew confused and pushed back from my workspace and left the office without informing anyone that I'd decided I was hungry and needed a snack.

However I did desire a firearm. One summer morning, mere days after my humiliating encounter with Wrangler, having arrived by train at the suburb I commuted to each morning, I had just settled down on a curb beside a steel safety rail rimming a small parking lot, where it was my habit to light a cigarette, drink the rest of my coffee, and read. Memory declines divulgence of that a.m.'s particular text but most likely it was Dostoevsky, as in those days Dostoevsky was all I ever read.

More than half of the cigarette remained when the first policeman preceded his partner by an instant, the bulky pair barging into my periphery, and asked to see some form of identification. I checked the page-number of my book—I remember the terror with which I endeavored to draw this action out, evincing all the languid insouciance I could muster, even willing myself to conduct a leisurely search of my pockets for a page marker before responding, aiming to communicate my utter indifference to this sudden incursion of The Law, meanwhile, clenching my fists to conceal the trembling fingers—and how nonetheless I fumblingly dropped the book (it was Fyodor, I see it now: a minor late work, lacking the lunatic rage of the unpolished younger scribe) so that several corners were bent and some mud marred the previously pristine pages (infuriatingly: I always labored to keep my books clean; the more wear incurred, the less likely I was to finish, though my sloth and poor attention to detail invariably led to spills, creased covers, crumbs in gutters, something—one reason I began so many books but rarely finished any, the other reason being that I lacked discipline, a personal deficiency I found a perpetual torment until I discarded altogether my indebtedness to your "discipline," your striving, your will to power, Reader, Brother, Servant, Fool) and I was ultimately too nervous to protract my show of pretending to search for a bookmark.

"What you doing," the first officer asked.

The actual answer to the man's question was banal: I was delaying my arrival at work by the fifteen-to-twenty minutes I knew I could accomplish without risk of being fired—in truth, without even being reprimanded, which I probably feared far more than actually losing my job at the office (it was still unclear what I was being paid to do there; on recent days I'd been conscripted by a different supervisor to carry boxes from one end of the office complex to the other. What was in these boxes? Nothing! I myself had assembled them a few days back at a different supervisor's behest; then left them, as directed, in a corner which must have fallen into the sector of this second supervisor [I couldn't keep straight who was senior to whom], who didn't want the boxes there, so that perhaps my services were being deployed in a passive-aggressive intra-office feud, I had no idea, and didn't much mind, as I enjoyed building the boxes, enjoyed the leisurely cross-office stroll bearing empty boxes after a quick pull from the soda bottle I kept filled with soda and wine, my empty head filling with visions of vapid satisfactions—the next bottle of wine awaiting me at home, a sangria or two to go with my sandwich and chips; the flanks of the ample Dominican secretary I'd imagine mounting while I masturbated in the men's room most days during the afternoon's pre-coffee lull; of course I still sorted stacks of papers whose purport I couldn't begin to parse, now with considerable skill: into alphabetical, numerical, or any other order and handed the files back to whichever supervisor or superior [every other employee in the office was technically my "superior," as far as I could tell] had handed them to me).

"Reading?" I said.

Neither officer was on edge, as he would have been had I posed an actual criminal threat; probably they'd been annoyed by the shrill housewife's housecall, perhaps this wasn't the first time she'd abused her citizen's right to be protected and served. Neither officer looked alert to or even prepared for the remote possibility for example, that in the time-abraded duffel beside me, instead of gym clothes and several of the books I'd begun that week, along with the journal in which I kept both my "notes" and my forays from the period into philosophy and theory, (the entire pathetic oeuvre of which, cold and wise with gin one evening not so long ago, I thankfully burned), but just imagine instead of these harmless materials, in this bag of ragged canvas, just below the topmost tanktop there lay: a handgun? Probably I could kill both of them, or at least one, firing at zero range for the face or chest, before either could reach his own piece.

The first of the two men repeated his request to see some sort of ID, which I unhesitatingly withdrew my wallet to flip through a deck's worth of unnecessary cards and receipts and search for, despite my sense that there was no clear reason why I should have to ID myself, as the only thing I was doing was reading on a curb reading one of Dostoevsky's lesser late novels, smoking a cigarette.

But what if I had a gun! I reiterate: what attracted me to the notion was not the premise that I might actually withdraw the handgun and with it claim these public-servants' lives, but that, were there a gun in my bag just now, I could, that is I would have it in my power to do so. Unbeknownst to them I could harbor this secret potency just out of sight, and these avatars of the Law would never know that whether they lived or died today was entirely in my hands, so that the fate of an entire accretion of experience, memory, hope, fear, "thought," perhaps a wife, a child, children, a whole family tree's destiny might hang in the balance, might hinge on whether or not I liked the man's tone, which I certainly didn't—and he, all the while never aware of anything more than a vague desire to get this shit over with already because he'd only had time for a bagel and coffee this morning, and that'd been a while back.

Of course, if there were a gun in my bag, I would even now run the risk of either officer asking offhand, "What's in the bag, Chief," and, sensing something off in my unwillingness to divulge, suggest I let him have a look, upon which investigation I would be either arrested or shot, depending on whether I made any subsequent threatening moves. But even this prospect thrilled me, so that when one of the cops now actually did ask what I had in the bag, Chief, I attempted to slide into what I imagined would be a guilty look, hoping to arouse his suspicion, but was only able to appear abject or cringing or servile, since this is the only mood my face ever honestly reflects, and thus unable to arouse any suspicion: precisely because, I instantly saw, there really was no gun in the bag. So that even as the policeman, whose radio had suddenly crackled, whined, and produced a coded bark, dismissed me with a wave, actually flipped my driver's license to the pavement as he spun and hustled off with his partner, presumably summoned now to a genuine threat to civic peace, I vowed that the next time I would have a gun in the bag.

That evening I visited a local megastore with the vague idea that I'd price automatic weapons. But I still couldn't get past certain crass, lower-order concerns: Assuming I could muster the money, not to mention the requisite licensing paperwork, to purchase a suitable firearm or arsenal, whom, exactly, would I want to shoot? The vision of absolute, unexercised power I'd almost seen flickered, and all I could think of was the mechanism of the gun. Could I really hold it to the temples of the Wranglers of the world, the fraternity-men, cops, Henry L. Winston-Trucks? Could I hold them responsible for failing to know me? Was any one of them worthy of blame? I might as well fire off round upon round at the sky.

Instead of a gun, I purchased a guitar—cheaply made, a pathetic little instrument—and went out to the parking lot where most of the spaces were empty or occupied by shopping carts only. I began to sing a song I composed on the spot, though the tune was not original, the chord-progression generic, derivative of the worst campfire pop (but of course I'd never actually been by a campfire, never submitted to that suffocating mood of commune and peace, the violent goodwill that will perhaps be embarrassing in the daylight, certainly nothing you can evaluate with logic, but that, nevertheless, under the night's diamond-studded dark cloth, at the outskirts of a central flickering warmth, surely all makes its own kind of sense? A shared understanding that all is well? I imagined this was the mechanism of camp), these are the words as well as I can remember them (even now, even here, I continue to spew lies: of course I remember the words! They are etched in my heart):

> I want to see my name
> inscribed in galaxies
> I want to have
> and unreturnable serve,
> But most of all
> I want to be
> more loved than I deserve:
> Is — thaaaat — too — much — to — ask?

I sang this song as loudly as I could until from the window of a passing pickup with lumber stacked in the bed came a flying bottle of Rolling Rock—half full of still-cold beer, the weight of which was sufficient to punch a second hole in the body of my just-bought "guitar."

"No!" I screamed, leaping to my feet as if to chase down the truck and my unseen assailants, though secretly relieved to see them accelerating in a spume of shrieking gravel out from that overlit megalot outside the megastore, since I have always been terrified of confrontations between men.

After I'd subsequently gone howling into the megastore parking lot's waste of sodium-perforated night; after that episode of shrill (albeit relieved) outrage and despair; after with head back I'd howled lupine peals that faintly traced the arc of the tune I could no longer accompany with the cheap "guitar," under an absent moon too indifferent to make a mocking cameo; after I'd stomped repeatedly on the "guitar" and hurled splintered chunks as far as they would go, which was scarcely more than a meter since the ostensible "wood" was an absurdly aerate dreck, and I was anyway weak; after I'd salvaged a copper-wound "E" string, noosed it round my neck and wildly searched for a suitable gallows substitute (nothing); after I'd lost myself in Keatsian contemplation of the iridescent sprinklings of emerald gold and diamond dust, the powdered glass all aglitter under cones of man-concocted light down that sparkling asphalt plain; after I pretended not to hear the jeering of a teenaged chieftain and his pack of teenaged droogs, flipped them a brazen finger once they'd passed from view beyond a parallel aisle of cars; after I stomped on the "guitar" some more, I began wandering indirectly toward the stop of the bus that would take me home, not wanting to go home, not wanting to be here either, or anywhere, when I was overcome by a sensation of vacancy, as the emotional display had somehow gutted me, as if I'd spilled something essential into the night, only to no purpose—or for precisely the purpose of creating a diversion for the passing cretins in their pickup truck (surely they'd been seeking someone to hurl a bottle or two of beer at, perhaps without even knowing what they sought; I had consummated their evening, even now they were probably packed onto a natty sofa in some infested hole draining additional bottles of Rolling Rock, competing to have their own version of the brief-but-still-funny episode heard above the familiar harmonic phrasings of, say, Modest Mouse). I remembered the description given me, some several years back, of what might have happened had my rotting appendix not been removed, as the doctors informed me, no more than an hour or so before it would have burst: Had it burst, they'd explained, its putrefaction would have spilled out into the surrounding abdominal region, polluted it, the resulting contamination requiring months of convalescence: the salience being that this rotted little bodily fruit needed to be harvested whole and intact, lest the poison it contained spill out and taint its whole surrounding milieu. The image dominated my reflection on the embarrassing display I'd provided all those megastore patrons. I was pleased with the analogy's aptness; I wondered how I would ever get all of that soul-rotting filth out intact.

I wandered in a state of high rumination—literally, as it is my habit to chew at the cudlike insides of my cheeks, which are (or were, until gluttony was shucked along with a panoply of other appetites in the riot of liberation that attended my personal ascent) hideously plump, as if stuffed with the pulped but unswallowed mastication of a long-completed meal—brooding, attempting to drift in an unscripted melancholy trance, guided only by the mute meditation on my failures as a man, but failing even in this—since despite my conscious desire to lapse into a fugue of pure feeling (which desire I wished would itself be unconscious) in which I'd wander the deserted streets like a Jeremiah of our age, seeing in his own frailty a signal or code, a message from on high, in the singular piteousness of my state, a universal sign: I will show you fear, I recited, knowing full well I was reciting (and in fact, remembering, despite my yearning to obliterate every last granule of humiliating memory, the way I had once—or actually much more than once, to be honest, quite often, almost nightly, I just did this an evening or so back—as a young man solemnly recited these lines, in their entirety, while peering through the weak-second of my half-reflected self, superimposed over the branches of a weeping willow, out my darkened bedroom window, my best approximation of what I conceived of as melancholy or tristesse [at the time I would of course have lacked access to the term] transfiguring my mien, meanwhile imagining a cinematic eye gazing down on this grief-stricken tableau, a somber swelling score, plaintive strings sweetly singing in a minor key, or perhaps the peal of bells, the young man's soul infused with lyrical light, at the heart of the silence, as the camera pulled up into the sky, drifting higher, gradually to reveal . . . well there was nothing more to be revealed: enough that the stricken audience perceive the affliction in the young man's gaze, What outsized feeling, what an immensity of soul, they would whisper to themselves— or not whisper, merely feel, in a wordless ecstasy of tidal pathos, my sacrificed lifeblood infusing the thirsty hearts of a million other desolate souls with something like hope, as the screen faded to credits [which would consist of a single name] the rising violins graced with the hiccups and sobs of grief-cracked women and men, all of them swimming in me, allowed, in an epiphanic moment, my gift to them, to truly see), wishing that for just one moment I might be guided by forces greater than my own confusion and woe, that for just this once I might feel closing around me the fists of divine wind suffusing the cosmos with mystery and miracle, feel myself tugged and carried along by the magnets and currents of fate, or the gods...

But despite this yen to lose myself, I'd been unable to forget where I lived (and likewise unable to forget my mother's habit of chewing an apple too close to my ear, of the dusty sunlight in the silent afternoons, of my basement's damp smell), or in what direction I needed to walk in order to get there, so that at each intersection instead of being carried by the winds of fate I was lucidly, horribly conscious of whether I was getting nearer to or farther from "home."

At last I found a sparsely populated bar and started ordering shots of Jack.

All of which I present by way of explanation. How it could have been that I was weaving between derelict vehicles parked or abandoned on an unfamiliar alleylike street—I'd succeeded in failing to know where I was—humming the same tune I'd been bellowing in the megastore lot some several hours back—which episode now, in my stupor, struck me as something stupendous, magnificently right, the only time in a very long time that I'd finally gotten to the heart of things, and I'd let a Ford F150-ful of fools ruin it with one hurled bottle. As I tottered between carhusks along pavement glittering with moonstruck glass I resolved (aloud) to return to the megastore the following day, where I would purchase a real guitar, assuming the megastore offered real guitars, bring it out with me into the parking lot, climb into the bed of a different pickup truck, commence booming out the same song I'd improvised that evening, even though I had no money for a second guitar and couldn't borrow any more from my old poor mom. And the point of the song (which I now realized I hadn't made up: I'd actually grafted the single verse onto a tune I'd stolen verbatim from a popular rock ballad I'd been particularly moved by as an adolescent and had earlier heard on one of the stereos on sale in the megastore's electronics department), if the song'd had a point, was its visceral power, which was of course gone.

I heard the sound but failed to grasp its significance until several moments had passed. Down the sidestreet from which it had seemed to issue—I imagined I could almost hear or feel a still-lingering reverberation—there was no one to be seen; the wind rustled the hairs on my arms, lifted a few pages of an abandoned morning paper; I saw streaks of moonlight kiss a rusted Mustang's metal husk, I saw paths of still more broken glass, a smokestack performing its appointed task (its smoke an almost lucent violet-gray), and the alley gave off of an avenue, down which I could see the skyline in the distance under a thick bank of clouds so low the half-towers looked like rigid charcoal fingers pressed through a fingerless glove, reaching down to rummage idly through the rubble of city life, and fleet footsteps echoed, fading with urgency toward the traintracks, which rose at this alley or sidestreet's far end, the report beginning to signify, I began to see its shape, like an afterglow of sound, as I shuffled into the alley, scanning the pavement intently, already starting to sober up.

CONTRIBUTORS

JONATHAN CALLAHAN's first book, *The Consummation of Dirk*, has been selected by Zachary Mason as the winner of this year's Starcherone Prize for Innovative Fiction and will be published in the fall of 2012. Stories and essays can be found or are forthcoming in *Unsaid, Witness, The Lifted Brow, Pank, Used Furniture Review, >kill author, Fringe, Fiction Writers Review,* and *The Collagist*.

ADAM COGBILL's writing has appeared or is forthcoming in *The Kenyon Review, Word Riot, The Ampersand, The Common,* and other publications, and he has been nominated for a Pushcart Prize. He lives in Northampton, MA.

NATE LIEDERBACH is the author of *Doing a Bit of Bleeding* and the Managing Editor of the *University of Utah's Western Humanities Review*. His work has appeared in, among other journals, *Versal, Mississippi Review, H_NGM_N, Corium Magazine, South Dakota Review,* and *Alice Blue Review*. He was recently chosen as a Best New Poet 2011.

SARAH MALONE's fiction has appeared or is forthcoming in *PANK, Open City, The Good Men Project,* and elsewhere. She blogs at www.sarahwrotethat.com

KATE PETERSEN's writing has appeared in *New England Review, The Iowa Review, The Los Angeles Review, The Rumpus, The Collagist,* and elsewhere. Her interview with James Salter recently appeared at *The Paris Review Daily*. She lives and studies in Minneapolis.

KAREN PITTELMAN's poems have been published in *Blip, New South*, and *The Pinch*, among other places. She is also the author of two non-fiction books about social justice philanthropy from Soft Skull Press. She lives in Brooklyn where she works as a writing coach and sings sad songs in a country band.

FRED SASAKI values your feedback and suggestions.

MATHIAS SVALINA is the author of one book of poems, *Destruction Myth* (Cleveland State Poetry Center), one book of prose, *I Am A Very Productive Entrepreneur* (Mud Luscious Press), & numerous chapbooks. With Zachary Schomburg he edits *Octopus Magazine* & Octopus Books.

KATE WYER works as a mental health interviewer for the public health care system of Baltimore. She enjoys her job. She writes about dogs, cooking, films and gardening at Moving Sidewalks.

Made in the USA
Charleston, SC
07 February 2012